P9-DEL-155

Charles Brockden Brown

Revised Edition

Twayne's United States Authors Series

Pattie Cowell, Editor

Colorado State University

TUSAS 98

Charles Brockden Brown
Courtesy of the Independence National Historical Park Collection

Charles Brockden Brown

Revised Edition

Donald A. Ringe

University of Kentucky

Twayne Publishers

A Division of G. K. Hall & Co. • Boston

Charles Brockden Brown, Revised Edition
Donald A. Ringe

Published by Twayne Publishers
A division of G. K. Hall & Co.
70 Lincoln Street
Boston, Massachusetts 02111

Copyediting supervised by Barbara Sutton.
Book production by Janet Z. Reynolds.
Book design by Barbara Anderson.
Typeset by Compositors Corp., Cedar Rapids, Iowa.

First published 1991.
10 9 8 7 6 5 4 3 2 1

The paper used in this publication meets the minimum requirements of American National Standard for Information Sciences—Permanence of Paper for Printed Library Materials, ANSI Z39.48-1984. ∞™

Printed and bound in the United States of America.

Library of Congress Cataloging-in-Publication Data

Ringe, Donald A.
Charles Brockden Brown / Donald A. Ringe. — Rev. ed.
p. cm. — (Twayne's United States authors series ; TUSAS 98)
Includes bibliographical references (p.) and index.
ISBN 0-8057-7606-0
1. Brown, Charles Brockden, 1771–1810—Criticism and interpretation. I. Title. II. Series.
PS1137.R56 1991
813′.2—dc20 90-45824

For

Don and Beth, Jim and D

Contents

Preface

In the twenty-five years or so that have passed since the first edition of this book was written, the study of Charles Brockden Brown has advanced markedly. In 1963 modern interest in Brown's novels was just beginning. The biographies by Harry R. Warfel and David Lee Clark had already been published, but only a handful of articles had appeared in the professional journals, and no scholarly edition of Brown's works had been prepared. Since then at least two major books on Brown have been published, new articles on his works appear every year, and the bicentennial edition of *Novels and Related Works* has provided us with texts edited in accordance with modern textual principles. Each volume contains, moreover, textual and historical essays that provide valuable information on the composition, publication, and critical reception of the book under discussion. Although we still lack an edition of the letters and need a more up-to-date biography, the study of Charles Brockden Brown has reached a high professional level.

During the intervening years, I too maintained an interest in Brown and his works. I prepared an essay on him for *Major Writers of Early American Literature* (1971), included a chapter on his novels in my *American Gothic: Imagination and Reason in Nineteenth-Century Fiction* (1982), and wrote the historical essay for the bicentennial edition of *Clara Howard* and *Jane Talbot* (1986). In the course of this work, I increased my knowledge and sharpened my understanding of Brown's novels. Because so much had been done over these years, I welcomed the opportunity to prepare a new edition of my book. I have rewritten or substantially revised parts of all seven chapters to reflect both what I have learned from other scholars and what I have discovered myself by rereading the books and thinking again about the problems they pose. I have added some notes and revised others to direct readers to pertinent recent scholarship, and I have provided an updated bibliography of secondary sources.

Despite these changes, the original purpose of the book remains unaltered. Though it recognizes the importance of Brown's novels as the first truly significant ones to be written in America and points out some of the ways in which they foreshadow later American fiction, it is not a historical study. Though it includes information about Brown's life, it is not a biography. It does not seek to view the man or his works in terms of some modern concept or theory, nor does it attempt to place them in the context of some broadly conceived theme. It offers, instead, a detailed analysis of the novels Brown wrote between 1798 and 1801, the period of his intense artistic creation. Five of the seven chapters are devoted to them. What went before and after is summarized in the opening and closing ones. The purpose remains, therefore, fundamentally critical: to understand and evaluate the books so that we may justly estimate Brown's success as a writer of fiction.

My debt to those who have shared my interest in Brown and his novels will be apparent in both the text and the notes. Special thanks are due, however, to John T. Hubbell, director of the Kent State University Press, for permitting me to quote extensively from all six volumes of the bicentennial edition of *The Novels and Related Works of Charles Brockden Brown,* the only one suitable for scholarly use.

Chronology

1771 Charles Brockden Brown born 17 January in Philadelphia.

1781–1786 Attends Friends' Latin School in Philadelphia until 1786 or 1787.

1787–1793 Studies law in the office of Alexander Wilcocks, but abandons the profession in 1793 before he has practiced it. Member of the Belles Lettres Club. Publishes "The Rhapsodist," a series of four essays, in the Philadelphia *Columbian Magazine* in 1789. Meets Elihu Hubbard Smith, who had come to Philadelphia in 1790–91 to study medicine.

1793–1796 During the Philadelphia yellow fever epidemic of 1793, visits Smith in Connecticut. In 1794 visits in New York, where Smith is practicing medicine. Becomes acquainted with the members of the Friendly Club, especially William Dunlap, whom he visits in Perth Amboy in 1795 and 1796. Writes a poem called "Devotion" in 1794. Begins a "Philadelphia novel"—possibly the beginning of *Arthur Mervyn*—in 1795. Moves to New York in the late summer of 1796.

1797 Returns to Philadelphia in March. Probably begins *Sky-Walk,* which he completes by March 1798, but the novel is never published.

1798 Publishes a number of short pieces, including the beginning of *Arthur Mervyn* in the Philadelphia *Weekly Magazine.* Publishes *Alcuin,* parts 1 and 2, in April. Arrives in New York for an extended visit in July. Publishes *Wieland* in September. Withdraws to Perth Amboy after Smith's death from yellow fever and his own illness with the disease. Leaves for Philadelphia in October and returns to New York in November.

1799 Publishes *Ormond* in January, and the first part of *Arthur Mervyn* by spring. In April begins to publish the *Monthly Magazine and American Review.* The first volume of *Edgar Huntly* is published in the summer and the complete book by the end of the year.

1800 Publishes the second part of *Arthur Mervyn* in the summer and the last issue of the *Monthly Magazine* in December. Returns to Philadelphia late in the year and becomes associated with his brothers' mercantile business.

1801 Publishes *Clara Howard* in June and *Jane Talbot* in December. Tours the Hudson to Albany and returns through Massachusetts and Connecticut.

1803 Is engaged in political pamphleteering: publishes *An Address to the Government of the United States, on the Cession of Louisiana to the French* in January; *Monroe's Embassy, or, the Conduct of the Government, in Relation to Our Claims to the Navigation of the Missisippi* in March. In October, begins to publish the *Literary Magazine and American Register,* which he continues to edit at least through 1806. Publishes *Carwin* in this magazine, 1803–5.

1804 Marries Elizabeth Linn 19 November; they have three sons and one daughter. Publishes a translation of Volney's *A View of the Soil and Climate of the United States.*

1805 Publishes "A Sketch of the Life and Character of John Blair Linn," his wife's brother, as an introduction to Linn's poem, *Valerian.*

1806 The mercantile firm is dissolved.

1807 Publishes a political pamphlet, *The British Treaty.* Begins to publish *The American Register, or General Repository of History, Politics, and Science,* of which five semiannual volumes appear between 1807 and his death.

1809 Publishes a political pamphlet, *An Address to the Congress of the United States, on the Utility and Justice of Restrictions upon Foreign Commerce,* in January.

1810 Dies 21 February in Philadelphia.

1815 *Alcuin,* parts 3 and 4, and *Stephen Calvert* are published in Dunlap's *Life of Charles Brockden Brown.*

Chapter One
Prelude

In a truly astonishing burst of creative energy, Charles Brockden Brown quickly established himself as a significant American writer and then abandoned his career. Writing at what must have been a high degree of intensity, he completed and published in four years all of the work for which he is remembered today: *Wieland* in 1798; *Ormond,* the first part of *Arthur Mervyn,* and *Edgar Huntly* in 1799; *Stephen Calvert,* published serially in the *Monthly Magazine and American Review* in 1799 and 1800; the second part of *Arthur Mervyn* in 1800; and *Clara Howard* and *Jane Talbot* in 1801. Any consideration of Brown as a literary artist must therefore concentrate on this remarkable period. Everything before was prelude; what remained was largely anticlimax. To be sure, Brown had been writing for many years before the publication of *Wieland.* His first published work, a poem and a series of four undistinguished essays, had appeared as early as 1789,[1] and he continued to write—magazine material, political pamphlets, and volumes of annals—almost to the time of his death at the age of thirty-nine in 1810. But from the point of view of American literary history, only the novels have any real importance. Only they command the attention of the serious student of American literature.

Critical Estimates

There can be no question that Brown's work is historically significant, for it marks the starting point of American fiction. Nothing like *Wieland* or *Edgar Huntly* had yet appeared in America, and it was almost a generation before any other American novelist would again write so much and so well. Brown stands virtually alone at the beginning of the nineteenth century, for only Hugh Henry Brackenridge among contemporary American novelists enjoys much critical esteem, and Brown's importance is surely the greater because he foreshadows so much of what was to come. Critics have seen in his work adumbrations of many other American writers, and Cooper, Hawthorne, and Poe are most frequently said to have been in his debt. Indeed, recent scholars have gone even further. Richard

Chase has seen in "Brown's elevated rhetoric and his melodramatic effects" a forecast of "much that is admirable" in later American writers of fiction, including "Melville, Faulkner, and even James."[2] And R. W. B. Lewis finds in the character of Arthur Mervyn the first appearance of a "representative hero" who was to recur in the works of many subsequent American authors.[3] Clearly Brown's novels demand attention if only because of their importance in the development of American literary art.

Historical significance, however, is not their only claim to our attention. Many readers have attested to their literary value. Writers as diverse as Keats, Shelley, Cooper, Poe, Prescott, Hawthorne, Whittier, and Margaret Fuller have admired his fiction;[4] and critics generally agree that the best of Brown's novels show his great, but unrealized, talent. Admittedly all of his books contain serious flaws, yet they have their strengths as well. The breathless pace of the best of his narratives, the taut suspense he was able at times to maintain, the sense of immediacy he could instill in some of his episodes, the convincing depiction of abnormal mental states, the verisimilitude of the scenes that are laid in plague-ridden Philadelphia—all are elements worthy of critical praise. They go a long way, moreover, in helping to mitigate the glaring faults in plotting, characterization, and style that would surely destroy the artistic effect entirely, if his books did not also generate such utterly absorbing interest. Brown's novels cannot be dismissed, therefore, as having only historical importance. The best of them still live, and, as a number of critics have testified, they can yet be read for their real—if limited—literary value.

Although there is general agreement on the importance and worth of Brown's achievement, opinion is curiously divided about the relative merits of individual books and the general thematic meaning of his fiction. Each of the novels, for example, has had its defenders. *Wieland,* of course, is generally considered to be the most successful, and *Edgar Huntly* is usually ranked second. Yet George Snell believes that *Arthur Mervyn* is best and dismisses the whole framework of *Edgar Huntly* as "entirely incredible."[5] Leslie A. Fiedler, on the other hand, considers *Edgar Huntly* "the most successful and characteristic of his gothic romances,"[6] Martin S. Vilas puts *Ormond* forward as Brown's "best work,"[7] and Paul Witherington writes that *Clara Howard* and *Jane Talbot* are "Brown's most mature novels."[8] Most critical attention, of course, has been directed to *Wieland, Arthur Mervyn,* and *Edgar Huntly,* but with each of these books, critics have advanced widely divergent interpretations. Some, for example, see Arthur Mervyn as an innocent, others as a self-serving character.[9] Opinion is similarly divided on the meaning of Brown's themes. David Lee Clark believes that Brown's purpose in writing was to disseminate radical thought, while Alexander Cowie writes that Brown included in his fiction "radical doctrine which he did not necessarily endorse."[10]

Such a degree of critical confusion can be explained in a number of ways. Part undoubtedly derives from the fact that Brown never wrote a completely satisfactory novel. Since all of his works are imperfect, each is likely to be valued for a different reason, and one is chosen over another because of the critical predilection of the reader. One whose taste runs toward the realistic might well prefer the plague scenes of *Arthur Mervyn* to everything else that Brown wrote, but another whose primary interest lies in the psychological state of the characters will probably value *Wieland* or *Edgar Huntly* the highest. Disagreements of this sort can never be resolved, for they are caused by inevitable differences in taste. Others, however, deriving from a misjudgment of Brown or a misinterpretation of his novels can surely be settled by an examination of his background and a thorough analysis of his books. The view, for example, that Brown was the strong proponent of contemporary radical thought who wrote his novels to disseminate such doctrine must certainly be rejected if it can be shown that the themes of his books run sharply counter to much of that thought or that Brown himself was a far more complex person than this view might suggest.

Any interpretation of Brown, therefore, that seeks to resolve the critical disagreement his works have engendered must first go back to the man himself, his intellectual background and development, and concentrate finally on close analysis of his literary work. The initial stress on biography is inevitable, for the study of Brown's early life is most pertinent to the discussion of his art. Charles Brockden Brown put much of himself into his books. This is not to say that they are autobiographical in any strict sense of the word or that Brown should be identified with any of the characters through whom he projects his themes. The relation, one suspects, is far more subtle than that. An intellectually alert young man, Brown was much concerned with ideas, and there can be no question that he was deeply interested in the ones he expressed in his books. Indeed, two of his critics—Harry R. Warfel and R. W. B. Lewis—see an even more intimate relation between Brown's life and work, for both suggest that writing was for him a kind of therapy through which he came to grips with the problems that troubled him.[11] Be that as it may—and the suggestion is an alluring one—a review of Brown's early life is clearly in order.

Personal Background

Born to Quaker parents in Philadelphia on 17 January 1771, Charles Brockden Brown grew up a rather frail, bookish young man. He attended the Friends' Latin School, conducted by Robert Proud, until about his sixteenth year, and instead of going to college—higher education was generally frowned upon by Quakers—he was apprenticed to Alexander Wilcocks to study law. Brown, however, was already developing an interest in things literary. He planned three epic poems on the discovery of America and the conquests of Mexico and Peru, and he joined with a group of young men to form the Belles Lettres Club, the purpose of which was to improve the members' skill in writing and eloquence. Although Brown continued to study law until 1793,[12] he never practiced his profession; he argued with his family that he could not bring himself, on moral grounds, to become a defender of injustice or an advocate for a wrong cause. His family, though grieved, finally accepted his decision and allowed him freedom to pursue a literary career, probably because, as Warfel has observed, his health at this time fell into decline and he sank into one of his severe—and recurring—melancholy moods.[13]

More important, however, from the point of view of his subsequent literary career are the intellectual influences that he came under. The most significant one, no doubt, was his parents' Quakerism, which surely gave his mind the liberal bent that was to develop so strongly during his early manhood.[14] His wide but undisciplined reading, moreover, undoubtedly confirmed this inclination. Since his father, Elijah Brown, read such works as William Godwin's *Political Justice,* Mary Wollstonecraft's *French Revolution,* and Robert Bage's *Man As He Is* when they appeared,[15] we can assume that Charles Brockden Brown grew up in a family conversant with contemporary ideas. We know that by 1792 he had been strongly influenced by Jean-Jacques Rousseau and had planned a work of fiction, "The Story of Julius," in imitation of him.[16] Sometime thereafter Brown himself became acquainted with Godwin's *Political Justice* and *Caleb Williams,* and in 1795 he even began a "Philadelphia novel"—probably an early version of *Arthur Mervyn*—under Godwin's influence.[17] As his friend Elihu Hubbard Smith put it in a letter of 27 May 1796, the influence of Rousseau had been unfortunate, but "*Godwin came, & all was light.*"[18]

Brown was undoubtedly influenced toward radicalism by Smith, a young deist who arrived in Philadelphia in the summer of 1790 to study medicine and whom Brown met sometime during his stay. Brown paid a number of visits to his new friend, first in Connecticut in 1793 and later in New York, where, in 1794, he became acquainted with members of the Friendly Club, to which Smith belonged. Brown attended meetings of this society when visiting Smith and his other friends in that city. Here he could take part in serious conversation on important issues of the day with the group of young Federalists who made up its membership.[19] Among them was William Dunlap—playwright, painter, eventual historian of both American art and American drama, and biographer of Brown—who, with Smith, became an intimate friend of the young Philadelphian. Brown was thus caught up in the intellectual current of the times, and he made the most of the experience. With Smith's and Dunlap's encouragement, he attempted to launch his literary career, and Smith in particular gave the greatest help by actually arranging the publication of Brown's initial book, parts 1 and 2 of *Alcuin,* a dialogue on the rights of women.

The history of *Alcuin: A Dialogue* is quite complex. The first two parts may have been written as early as the fall or winter of 1796 or as late as the summer of 1797. These parts of the book were published twice in the spring of 1798. Before Smith's New York edition appeared on 27 April, Brown had already published a somewhat altered version in the Philadelphia *Weekly Magazine* between 17 March and 7 April. When Smith discovered what Brown was doing, he enjoined him from publishing any more of the book until the edition appeared in New York. Brown quickly sent him the manuscript of parts 3 and 4, which may have been written in 1797, but when Smith read them, he doubted the expediency of publishing until he had sought the advice of some woman of "good-sense & candour."[20] These parts remained in manuscript, however, until they appeared in Dunlap's biography in 1815. All four parts of *Alcuin* were not published together until Lee R. Edwards prepared her edition of 1971.[21] Since then, the complete book has also appeared in a well-edited text as part of the bicentennial edition of Brown's major works.[22]

Although *Alcuin* is not a strong book from the point of view of literary value, it remains of interest as the first major publication of America's earliest professional novelist and provides an insight into Brown's mind at the beginning of his writing career. The book is simply a dialogue between Alcuin, a poor schoolmaster, and Mrs. Carter, a widow and "bluestocking." Some critics have seen touches of characterization in Brown's treatment of these two,[23] but neither is really well depicted. *Alcuin* is primarily important for the liberal ideas that Brown has them present. In part 1 Alcuin meets Mrs. Carter one evening at her brother's house and engages her in conversation. They discuss the position of women in society, with Alcuin defending the role they have been assigned and Mrs. Carter objecting that they are confined to too narrow a sphere. They are the victims of an inadequate education, she believes, and are excluded from those professions that would allow them to play an independent role in society. In part 2 the characters turn to politics and government. Here Mrs. Carter argues that the exclusion of women from the rights and duties of citizenship purely on the basis of sex is unjust.

In the third and fourth parts, Alcuin and Mrs. Carter discuss ideas that are much more radical. A week after their initial dialogue, he returns for a second visit and describes a visionary society—"the paradise of women" (6:34)—from which he pretends to have just returned. There, except for the obvious physical differences, the sexes are treated with complete equality. They dress in the same kinds of clothes, receive identical educations, and share equally in the tasks that must be performed in society. Marriage is unknown among them. At this point Alcuin's description of the utopian society is cut short, and he and Mrs. Carter engage in a discussion of marriage itself. She immediately perceives the source of Alcuin's imaginary society in the ideas of those thinkers who, in her words, "aim at the deepest foundation of civil society" (6:52), and she will not accept the conclusion toward which, she thinks, Alcuin's argument is tending. Firm in her support of the institution of marriage, she will not hear of its abolition. She believes, nonetheless, that in the current state of society, marriage laws and customs work an injustice on women, and she presents an extended argument for divorce.

We cannot assume, of course, that the ideas Brown presents through the characters in *Alcuin* are his own. That his reading during the 1790s introduced him to such radical thought is certain, and we know from a letter of 24 October 1795 to his friend Joseph Bringhurst that he argued vigorously at that time against the Christian religion yet remained open to his friend's defense of it.[24] Dunlap is certainly right when he reports that Brown had a "predisposition to scepticism," but he also observes that much of Brown's reading "tended to bewilder rather than enlighten" him so that like "many others, he imputed . . . the defects which are but too apparent in existing systems" to the wrong causes: the codes by which men live, instead of "the ignorance and selfishness of individuals." In most of this passage, Dunlap is paraphrasing Paul Allen, whose biography of Brown he revised and completed.[25] Allen also observed that "those plunging tenets and dangerous doctrines" that Brown advanced in *Alcuin* gradually changed as he mingled in society and observed manners. Ideas which "may be defended by an able logician in a thousand different ways are abandoned when he sees them brought to the touch of experiment and fail."[26]

Though we cannot trace in detail the evolution of Brown's thought, there is ample evidence to suggest that, although he was always fascinated with utopian schemes and even sketched utopian plans himself,[27] he turned away from the actual acceptance of them by the time he wrote his novels. Even in *Alcuin,* as we have seen, the liberal Mrs. Carter expresses her disapproval of contemporary radical thinkers, and in the novels that followed that book into print, Brown never lends his assent to utopian schemes. It is always the villainous characters—Carwin, Ludloe, and Ormond—who are the most strongly influenced by radical thought, and their actions are, without exception, productive of a multitude of evils against which the virtuous characters are forced to struggle. The entire action of *Ormond,* moreover, opposes many of the radical ideas that Brown picked up in his reading.[28] In the light of this evidence, one is reluctant to believe that Brown remained himself a proponent of such ideas. That they held an interest for him cannot be doubted, but it seems most reasonable to assume that he used them in his fiction for artistic rather than for propagandistic purposes.

To stress unduly the rationalist side of Brown's personality may lead to a misunderstanding of both the man and his work, for there was an element in his makeup that points in a different direction. For years Brown seems to have been afflicted with a strange emotional disorder. He fell into spells of melancholy that can only be called abnormal, and his letters reveal the depths of morbid self-criticism into which he sometimes slipped. Joseph Brown had apparently recognized this trait in his younger brother, for he stressed in his letters to him the importance of keeping one's "fears and anxieties" from the eyes of others. Brown revealed this fact in a letter to William W. Wilkins and went on to say that he failed to heed his brother's precept only with regard to Wilkins and one other person. Yet Brown does not reveal anything really specific even in letters to his closest friends. Instead he hints darkly at unspeakable mysteries. Thus, in his letter to Wilkins, he wrote: "what useful purpose could be answered by making C. B. B. better known to his friends? What but their unhappiness could be produced by it?" Indeed, he even writes of "that profound abyss of ignominy and debasement, into which I am sunk by my own reflections."[29]

Smith and Dunlap, too, received such letters from their friend, and Smith in particular wrote two long replies in May 1796 in which, playing the psychologist, he tries to talk Brown out of his strange affliction. He berates him soundly for being neither wholly reticent nor completely explicit in his self-revelation, and he attempts to bring him into a more healthy mental state.[30] His advice, however, seems to have done little permanent good. Nearly two years later, on 1 January 1798, Brown expressed, in a letter to Dunlap, such extremes of morbid self-consciousness and depths of self-abhorrence that Dunlap did not acknowledge it; he merely wrote on the manuscript his expression of regret that his beloved friend could sometimes write in such a manner.[31] The point must not be overstressed, for Brown should no more be viewed as a mental case than he should be seen as an utter rationalist. The evidence is important, nonetheless, in helping the critic to a balanced view of the man and in suggesting a possible source in Brown himself for that interest in human psychology so apparent in his fiction.

Charles Brockden Brown, it seems fair to conclude, was a complex person who cannot be simply or easily characterized. Intelligent, alert, greatly interested in contemporary ideas, he was also a man frequently ill in body and deeply troubled in mind. His very complexity, moreover, must surely have had an effect on his writing, and as we read we are increasingly drawn to the suggestion that the novels did indeed serve a therapeutic purpose for him—if not in curing his melancholy, at least in helping him clarify his thought. For Brown's views underwent a dramatic change during the course of a relatively few years. Obviously influenced by the rationalist thought of Godwin and others during the early stage of his career, Brown made his first attempt at novel writing in 1795 with what was presumably an imitation of *Caleb Williams,* and he published in *Alcuin* views that were certainly radical for his time. Yet in his final novel, *Jane Talbot,* published in 1801, Brown presents a much more conservative view. He specifically opposes Godwinian rationalism and affirms the value of religious faith as the guide to life. Though we cannot assume that Brown rejected entirely all he had read in his youth, the evidence clearly reveals that he changed his opinions considerably during the period of his intense artistic creation, and one is drawn to the view that, to some extent, the writing itself helped him to formulate his final intellectual position.

Fictional Method

Such an interpretation gains support from the manner in which the novels were written. We have it on Dunlap's authority that Brown did not make in advance an overall plan for a book but developed its form as he wrote: "He began to write a novel after having only determined upon one leading circumstance, character or idea, and trusted to the growth of one incident from another, and the appropriate sentiments from the incidents. One volume would be finished and printed before he had formed any plan for the beginning of the second, or any plan for the continuation, development or denouement of the story."[32] What happened in the process is well illustrated by the second part of *Arthur Mervyn*. Brown, we know, had made at least a general plan for the book before he began to write,[33] but he made some major changes as the work progressed. The character of Mrs. Achsa Fielding is not even mentioned in his original statement, yet she is the woman whom Mervyn eventually marries in the completed novel! Because of her presence, the story comes to a conclusion significantly different in meaning from what Brown had apparently first intended, a meaning that could have developed only while Brown was composing the book.[34]

An analysis of Brown's fictional method by W. B. Berthoff lends further weight to the hypothesis that Brown developed his themes in the course of the writing itself. Berthoff observes that Brown did not use narration merely to illustrate preconceived ideas; he made it, rather, "an instrument for *discovering* ideas, for exploring and testing them out." Thus, Berthoff argues, Brown did not set out to expound ideas in his books—not Godwin's or, indeed, his own—but put them to the test of action by contriving incidents in which the characters attempt to live by the concepts and put them into practice. Through a series of such incidents, each of which restates or deepens the central idea, a theme emerges that may be something quite different from the concepts explicitly stated in the book. The theme arises, therefore, from the total action of the story and at times seems to defy simple expression because it takes cognizance of the conflicts and contradictions in human nature and reflects the full complexity of human experience.[35]

It should be apparent, therefore, that the critic of Brown who hopes to arrive at a valid interpretation of the novels and at a just estimate of their literary worth must lay preconceptions aside and turn to the close analysis of the individual books. The task, of course, is complicated by a number of factors. Since the novels took form as he wrote them and probably did not develop according to any preconceived plan, readers are presented with obvious difficulties that are only compounded by the complex order of composition of the books themselves. According to Dunlap, Brown at one time had five novels going at once, [36] and there is no way now to determine the precise order of their development. *Arthur Mervyn,* for example, may have been begun as early as 1795, and the first nine chapters of it preceded *Wieland* in print, yet it stands in the order of publication as Brown's third novel. In a similar fashion, *Edgar Huntly* appeared as his fourth, but parts of it probably derive from his earliest and now lost novel, *Sky-Walk; or, The Man Unknown to Himself,* finished early in 1798.[37] Indeed, Brown sometimes even borrowed from his own writings, for the same or similar episodes occasionally appear in more than one work.[38]

Fortunately, however, the problem of chronological order need not concern us unduly, for Brown's career as a novelist—or at least the major part of it—was much too short to make the order of composition of overriding importance. Besides, there are other problems that demand our critical attention. In some important ways, Brown's fictional techniques foreshadow the devices of the modern novelist, and questions of interpretation in his books are sometimes those that we are familiar with from more recent fiction. The first-person method of narration by which most of his books are developed and the multiple point of view he employed in *Wieland* and *Arthur Mervyn* are cases in point. Although the devices certainly add to the interest of the novels, the complications of meaning that sometimes arise from their use make the books, like many modern ones, somewhat difficult to analyze. Readers, however, should not be deterred for that reason. The problem of interpretation can become an absorbing one, and the rewards to be obtained are substantial. Brown's books, at their best, contain much of artistic value, and, even at their worst, they add considerably to our understanding of many important developments in subsequent American fiction.

Chapter Two
Wieland

The publication of *Wieland; or, The Transformation* in 1798 marks the true beginning of Brown's literary career, for although he had already written both *Alcuin* and *Sky-Walk* and had published a number of minor pieces,[1] *Wieland* is the first of his major works to be published in its entirety. Deriving the central incident from an actual murder, an account of which had been published in both New York and Philadelphia in 1796,[2] Brown sketched an outline for the story in a notebook and most probably began writing early in 1798. Throughout the spring and summer, he discussed the book with his friends William Dunlap, Elihu Hubbard Smith, and William Johnson. Most of the manuscript was delivered to the printer on 25 July, but Brown was apparently still working on the conclusion—the ill-fated final chapter, perhaps—as late as 5 September.[3] The book was published on 14 September,[4] at the height of the yellow fever epidemic that had struck New York in August and, before it had run its course, was to take off Smith and force Brown himself, who was living in New York at the time and had contracted the disease, to move to Perth Amboy, New Jersey.

Composition and Purpose

In composing his novel, Brown drew upon many literary sources. It has long been known, for example, that Clara Wieland owes something to the sentimental heroines of Samuel Richardson; that the Gothic tone of the book, especially in those incidents that take place in Clara's room, derives from the romances of Ann Radcliffe and others; and that the mysterious but natural phenomena of the novel are related to similar devices in Friedrich von Schiller's *The Ghost-Seer* and Cajetan Tschink's *The Victim of Magical Delusion*.[5] It has also been suggested that Brown could have been influenced by Christoph Maria Wieland's *The Trial of Abraham* and by such popular books of the time as Eliza Parsons's *The Mysterious*

Warning or Karl Kahlert's *The Necromancer,* all of which bear certain similarities to *Wieland.*[6] There are many analogues in contemporary fiction for most of the elements to be found in Brown's novel—not only the mysterious voices but also such devices as the enclosures, the temple, the summerhouse, and Clara's bedroom and closet. Some critics have even found important similarities between Brown's novel and Shakespeare's *Much Ado about Nothing* and *Hamlet,* Milton's *Paradise Lost,* and the legend of Faust.[7]

Wieland is certainly more than a conventional Gothic novel. Other such works may rely on deceptive appearance to confuse or terrify the characters and may, like *Wieland,* attribute most of the bizarre incidents they contain to natural causes, but *Wieland* stands apart from them in its intense intellectuality, in its probing of the principles by which human beings direct their lives, and in the disaster that results from their misapprehensions of reality. At the intellectual core of the book is the sensationalist psychology of the time,[8] a position shared by all the major characters, who constantly seek meaning in the appearances that are presented to their senses but who are made in turn to perceive how wrong the inferences may be that they draw from experience. "The will is the tool of the understanding," Clara writes at one point, "which must fashion its conclusions on the notices of sense" (1:35), a succinct description of the psychology that lies at the heart of the book. But Brown uses his materials creatively to question this model of the human mind, and he leaves us with the impression that his probing has been deep and illuminating.

Brown's method in developing the book is that which Berthoff describes as his usual one.[9] The characters act in a series of analogous incidents that test the ideas by which they attempt to live, and the cumulative effect reveals the central theme. In *Wieland,* Brown creates a number of attractive and "enlightened" young people whose thoughts and actions, when they are confronted by unusual circumstances, unmistakably demonstrate what Brown is about in his book. The group centers on the Wieland family: Theodore, a studious young man with a certain Calvinistic streak in his intellectual makeup; his wife, Catharine; and their four children. Clara Wieland, who idolizes her brother and has shared his education, lives but a short distance away and is constantly in their company. A fourth member of the group is Catharine's brother, Henry Pleyel, a lighthearted young rationalist who frequently comes to visit them. The Wielands live an almost idyllic existence in semirural isolation on the banks of the Schuylkill, but there is an important element in their past from the influence of which they can never escape, and an unexpected and unforeseen future waits to test them severely.

Background to the Action

Always in the background lies the history of the elder Wieland, the father of Theodore and Clara. The son of a disinherited German nobleman, he is apprenticed to a London merchant, who works him long and hard. Somewhat morose and given to gloomy reflection, he is haunted by a nameless craving that is satisfied only when he chances upon a religious book and finds a theme for meditation. Guided by a Camisard tract he has read, he becomes increasingly introspective, constructs a private religion, develops an intensely scrupulous conscience, and labors "to keep alive a sentiment of fear, and a belief of the awe-creating presence of the Deity" (1:9). Convinced that he must disseminate his belief, he journeys to America to preach it to the Indians, a mission he tries to perform only after he has successfully established himself in the country for fourteen years.

Failing in his missionary work, however, he retires to his farm on the Schuylkill and increasingly isolates himself. He avoids all forms of social worship and even constructs a kind of temple "on the top of a rock whose sides were steep, rugged, and encumbered with dwarf cedars and stony asperities" where, in a space that was "without seat, table, or ornament of any kind," he worships his God alone each day at midnight and noon (1:11–12). He comes to believe, however, that he has failed to obey a command laid on him and that his offense is inexpiable. Foreseeing his approaching end, he goes alone to his temple at midnight. An eerie light appears; he is struck a heavy blow; his clothes are burned to ashes; and, after falling into fever, delirium, and a lethargic sleep, he later dies. Clara is six at the time, her brother about ten.

With the early death of their mother as well, the orphaned children are raised in accordance with "enlightened" principles. "By accident more than design," the maiden aunt who educates them mingles the proper amounts of indulgence and steadfastness in forming their characters, sees that they are properly "instructed in most branches of useful knowledge," and preserves them "from the corruption and tyranny of colleges and boarding-schools" (1:20), in those days in the hands of religious sects. The children's attitude toward religion is therefore much different from what their father's had been. Their "education had been modelled by no religious standard," for they were "left to the guidance of [their] own understanding, and the casual impressions which society might make upon

[them]" (1:22). How far they are removed from their father's state of mind is revealed in the use to which they put his temple once they are grown. No longer an isolated spot for austere and private worship, the temple is converted by the younger Wielands to social uses. They add a harpsichord and a bust of Cicero, objects indicative of their rational attitudes, and they retire to the place on summer evenings to sing, talk, read, and occasionally banquet.

The Wielands are not, however, without religion, but to Clara and Catharine it is merely "the product of lively feelings, excited by reflection on our own happiness, and by the grandeur of external nature. We sought not a basis for our faith, in the weighing of proofs, and the dissection of creeds. Our devotion was a mixed and casual sentiment, seldom verbally expressed, or solicitously sought, or carefully retained" (1:22). It does little more than heighten a pleasure that hardly seemed to require it. Wieland is very different. More deeply religious than his sister, he nonetheless attempts to find an intellectual basis for his belief: "He was much conversant with the history of religious opinions, and took pains to ascertain their validity. He deemed it indispensable to examine the ground of his belief, to settle the relation between motives and actions, the criterion of merit, and the kinds and properties of evidence." Though obviously resembling his father in his concern with religion, "the mind of the son," Clara glibly tells us, "was enriched by science, and embellished with literature" (1:23). Children of their age, they accept most of its assumptions and settle down to several pleasant years in their retreat.

Their retired society is made all the more pleasurable by the addition of Pleyel, a man whose "discernment was acute" but who "was prone to view every object merely as supplying materials for mirth." As well educated as Wieland, he is "not behind his friend in his knowledge of the history and metaphysics of religion." But Wieland is fundamentally a believer, and Pleyel is a complete rationalist. "The champion of intellectual liberty," he rejects "all guidance but that of his reason" (1:25) and denies faith "to any testimony but that of his senses" (1:75). In Pleyel, therefore, we have the "enlightened" man in test-tube purity, but he is not so different from Wieland that the two cannot get along. They frequently discuss their differences of opinion and manage their arguments with candor and skill. Indeed, their fundamental attitudes toward knowledge are not really so diverse as one might expect. Both are concerned with the analysis and evaluation of the available evidence. Their difference lies in their conclusions, for, "where one discovered only confirmations of his faith, the other could find nothing but reasons for doubt" (1:25). Their arguments are thus entirely friendly and do not detract at all from the pleasure each enjoys in the other's company.

The Wielands' pleasant life is suddenly disrupted when Brown introduces an element designed to put the characters' views to a serious test. One night, after a sudden shower drives the group from the temple, Wieland returns alone to pick up a letter inadvertently left there. He hears a voice that sounds like his wife's call out to him to stop because there is danger before him and to return to the house. Since the voice is heard under circumstances that make it impossible for it to have been Catharine's, Wieland is faced with the difficulty of drawing an inference from unaccountable sense impressions. Wieland, however, is not alone with this problem. Some three weeks later, as he and Pleyel talk alone in the temple at night, the rationalist Pleyel, who had dismissed the first voice as an illusion of the senses, hears it too and is forced to admit its reality. Clara too is eventually confronted with the phenomenon, for, still later, she hears mysterious voices whispering in her room late at night, and the whole household, finally, is awakened by a strange call when Clara, fleeing the voices in her room, faints at her brother's doorstep. All the characters, therefore, are compelled to interpret sense impressions that seem to have no easily discernible basis in reality and are at the very least ambiguous. By this means, Brown initiates the series of experiences that form the basic structure of the book and through which is revealed its central theme.

The problem the characters face is complicated by the fact that although most of the voices they hear are real, they are produced by a means that lies completely beyond their normal experience. They are the result of ventriloquism. A strange and ominous character named Carwin appears on the scene shortly after the trouble begins. A man of beautifully flexible voice and keen intellect, he soon is accepted into the little coterie, despite the unexplained mystery of his past. Pleyel had met him in Spain three years before under suspicious circumstances, and although the other characters are curious to know more about him, he avoids all mention of his background. Suffice it to say, the reader eventually learns that Carwin had early discovered in himself the ability to mimic other voices and to project them where he wished. Though he wants to avoid using the power after his return to America, he is trapped in the temple when Wieland approaches that fateful night, and to avoid being discovered, he is tempted to speak out in Catharine's voice. Once having succumbed to temptation, moreover, he uses his power on seven additional occasions. The other characters are completely unaware of Carwin's power, and they easily fall prey to his vocal tricks.

Pleyel and Wieland

The point of the matter is not that the characters are simply duped by Carwin, for Brown suggests that human beings are, at times, unable to draw the proper conclusions from more normal sensations as well. Surely if any one of the group should be able to make correct inferences from sensory data, it ought to be the rationalist Pleyel. Without the morbid family history of the Wielands and blessed with an excellent mind, Pleyel is careful in examining evidence and cautious in making judgments. Yet he too misinterprets his sensations and comes to completely unjustified conclusions about what he has seen and heard. He mistakes the expression on Clara's face when Carwin is present as love for the mysterious stranger; he considers her actions suspicious when he searches for her and finds her late at night in a secluded summerhouse; he misconstrues some words he catches sight of in her secret journal as referring to an assignation; and he believes without question that the voices he finally hears coming from the summerhouse mean that she and Carwin are carrying on an affair. He even misinterprets the footsteps he hears late that night as indicating her return from a clandestine meeting (1:121–35). All that he hears and sees is perfectly accurate. His senses correctly report the sights and sounds that have been generated. But in every case his mind makes an unjustified inference, and his imagination augments his error.

The innocent Clara is utterly appalled, therefore, when, convinced that his conclusion is beyond dispute, he confronts her with his accusation, because she realizes only too well that she must defend her name against witnesses they both believe to be "the most explicit and unerring, of those which support the fabric of human knowledge" (1:114). She is well aware that he places great faith in his sensory perception. "Evidence less than this," he tells her, "would only have excited resentment and scorn. The wretch who should have breathed a suspicion injurious to thy honor, would have been regarded without anger; not hatred or envy could have prompted him; it would merely be an argument of madness. That my eyes, that my ears, should bear witness to thy fall! By no other way could detestible conviction be imparted" (1:104). Pleyel's conclusion is utterly false, but once he has made up his mind, his opinion is hardly to be shaken. When Clara goes to his house to disabuse him of his error, he airily assumes that she comes as a repentant sinner, and although he occasionally has some misgivings, he recounts the evidence upon which his belief is based and ends their interview still firmly convinced of her infamy.

Pleyel, of course, should know better. His years of acquaintance with Clara and the intimate knowledge he has of her character and principles should have borne testimony to the falseness of his suspicions and made him at least question the evidence of his senses. Indeed, even Carwin, who projects the voices that Pleyel hears in the summerhouse, did not think that he could dupe the rationalist for long. He engaged in the task, as he later tells Clara, believing that the deception would soon be corrected. "When I think of your character," Carwin continues, "and of the inferences which this dialogue was intended to suggest, it seems incredible that this delusion should be produced" (1:210). Yet produced it was, and with far more effect than Carwin anticipated, for Pleyel had already misconstrued a number of Clara's words and actions before he heard the voices. The thoroughness of his delusion, therefore, clearly reveals the serious error in the rationalist theory by which Pleyel has attempted to live—its failure to take sufficiently into account that all human beings, no matter how rational, possess fallible minds and powerful passions. Though he admits "the limitedness of human faculties" (1:121), Pleyel seems unable to recognize his own fallibility when he succumbs to his passions.[10]

It is small wonder, then, that Wieland too fails at solving the problem, since he is influenced by far more sinister forces than any with which the less complex Pleyel has had to contend. The memory of his father's death forever lurks in his mind and always comes to the fore whenever he visits the temple alone or at night. It is thus already present on that fateful evening when Carwin first projects his imitation of Catharine's voice. The effect is immediate and profound. Always a grave and thoughtful person, Wieland becomes even more introspective after that experience, and his thoughts thereafter "were generally found to have a relation, more or less direct, with this incident." Since he had always considered his father's death "as flowing from a direct and supernatural decree" (1:35), it is not difficult for him to believe that the voice he has heard may derive from a supernatural source—a conclusion that predisposes him to hear additional commands. Hence, when later voices, not produced by Carwin, urge him to monstrous acts against his wife and children, Wieland, crossing the line between sanity and madness, obeys what he thinks is a divine command in killing them.

Yet Wieland is not so different from Pleyel as his madness might seem to indicate, for he is no less certain of his ability to arrive at truth through the interpretation of sensory evidence. When Pleyel tells him of his belief in Clara's guilt, Wieland does not think it possible for Pleyel to have been deceived. Nonetheless, he is willing to accept Clara's vindication of herself but only because long experience has attested to her veracity, and "nothing less than [his] own hearing and vision would convince [him], in opposition to her own assertions, that [his] sister had fallen into wickedness like this" (1:110). That he should refer to his senses in this way is ironic in view of Pleyel's error,[11] but Wieland is consistent in his acceptance of sensory evidence, and even in his homicidal mania, he believes he is acting as a perfectly reasonable man. Thus, when he recounts the events of the night on which he hears the voice order him to kill his wife, he describes the sequence rationally as a simple association of ideas. The happiness he feels in his love for his wife and children fills him with thoughts of gratitude to God, from whom his blessings flow, and gratitude leads him to thoughts of the service due so great a benefactor.

In a moment of exaltation, then, Wieland longs for "the blissful privilege of direct communication with [God], and of listening to the audible enunciation of [His] pleasure"; and he prays: "Would that a momentary emanation from thy glory would visit me! that some unambiguous token of thy presence would salute my senses!" (1:166–67). When he sees the vision and hears the voice that, shortly thereafter, commands him to kill his wife, he accepts what he sees and hears as valid sensory evidence. That this and the subsequent voices exist in his mind alone is clearly underscored in the book, but the point of the matter is that they seem real to him; he is thoroughly convinced of their objectivity. With Wieland, therefore, Brown is ringing a variation on the theme he developed in the character of Pleyel. The rationalist fails in interpreting true sensations accurately, but his friend is unable to distinguish between true and false sensations.

The implications of Wieland's experience, moreover, may have an even greater significance than is at first apparent, for Larzer Ziff has argued that it makes the most telling comment on the optimistic psychology that informs the book. Whereas Pleyel's errors may be dismissed as simply a temporary delusion of the individual, Wieland's suggest, in Ziff's analysis, a much more fundamental flaw in his condition. Early in the novel, after Wieland first hears what he thinks is Catharine's voice warning him from the temple, Clara analyzes the problem and states the question explicitly. She does not like to think that Wieland has suffered a delusion because it argues "a diseased condition of his frame, which might show itself hereafter in more dangerous symptoms. The will is the tool of the understanding, which must fashion its conclusions on the notices of sense. If the senses be depraved, it is impossible to calculate the evils that may flow from the consequent deductions of the understanding" (1:35). *Depraved,* Ziff believes, is the key word in the passage, for it implies that human nature is not so simple as contemporary psychology would have it. Wieland has, most likely, inherited his mania from his father. In Ziff's opinion, therefore, Wieland succumbs not to a simple delusion of the senses but to "an inherited depravity which preceded it," a view of human nature that with its strong Calvinistic overtones runs counter to the optimistic psychology of the day.[12]

Clara

Be that as it may, Brown's exploration of the problem does not end at this point. Pleyel and Wieland are not, after all, the central characters, for Brown merely uses them as background figures to illustrate most clearly the issue he is concerned with in the book. The focus of attention throughout the novel is on Clara.[13] She is the one who narrates the story to an unnamed person who apparently has the "right to be informed of the events that have lately happened in [her] family" (1:5). She is the primary target of many of Carwin's machinations. Hence, she is forced to confront problems similar to those that face Pleyel and Wieland and also to endure the consequences of their errors. All three are transformed by their experiences, but Clara's transformation is the most shattering. Pleyel is eventually disabused of his errors, and Wieland commits suicide when he finally learns that he has acted under a delusion. Clara, on the other hand, rejected by the man she loves and threatened by the brother she has loved and revered, is pushed into a state of insanity that seems not to have been completely cured even at the end of the book.

Although she resembles both Pleyel and Wieland in some of her mental attitudes, Clara is in many ways quite different from both. Like Pleyel, of course, she accepts the psychology of the time, but although she is generally averse to any supernatural explanation of strange events, she does eventually come to believe that the voices they hear are from a benevolent supernatural source. Like Wieland, moreover, she feels the strong influence of the past in the recurring memory of her father's death, and even as she writes she cannot yet decide whether the event should be assigned to a supernatural or a natural cause—whether her father died by the direct stroke of the divine hand, or, as Brown suggests, though he does not use the term, of "spontaneous combustion." Yet unlike her brother she engages in no brooding thoughts on religious matters but professes a rather vague, liberal religion. Deeply involved with problems in psychology, Clara seeks causes and explanations of all the strange phenomena that occur and ponders much on the problem of interpreting conflicting and ambiguous sensations. In the course of her musings, she stumbles on some phenomena for which she cannot rationally account.[14]

This process begins shortly after the appearance of Carwin, whom Clara first sees when he stops at the house to ask for a drink to quench his thirst. Impressed by the mellifluous voice she hears, she is surprised to find, when she sees his face, that he is strangely ugly. There are about him, however, signs that "betoken a mind of the highest order" (1:53). Unaccountably affected by the appearance of the man, she sketches his portrait, and sitting alone in her apartment the following dark and stormy day, she gazes at it until her mind becomes "absorbed in thoughts ominous and dreary." Even when she turns fondly to the images of her brother and his children, "they only increased the mournfulness of [her] contemplations." The smiles of the children are as bland as ever and the brow of the father as dignified, but for some inexplicable reason she thinks of them "with anguish" (1:54). As yet, nothing has occurred to connect the mysterious Carwin with any of the unusual events. Indeed, she has seen him only briefly and has not yet spoken to him at all. Yet, somehow, her mind has made a connection between the curious stranger and her own beloved family.

This incident is not the only instance of a strange process in Clara's mind. Some weeks later, after "a toilsome day," Clara goes alone to her summerhouse on the bank of the river to recoup her spirits depressed "through the fatigue of long attention." "The lulling sounds of the waterfall," the fragrance of the honeysuckle, and the gathering dusk of evening succeed in becalming her spirits, and in a short time she falls asleep. Her dreams, however, are anything but peaceful. After some incoherent episodes, she finds herself, in the twilight of evening, approaching her brother's house, unaware of a pit that lay in her path. "As I carelessly pursued my walk," she writes, "I thought I saw my brother, standing at some distance before me, beckoning and calling me to make haste. He stood on the opposite edge of the gulph. I mended my pace, and one step more would have plunged me into this abyss, had not some one from behind caught suddenly my arm, and exclaimed, in a voice of eagerness and terror, 'Hold! hold!' " (1:61–62). Clara suddenly starts awake, only to hear a mysterious voice warn her away from that spot. Elsewhere, it informs her, she will be safe, but here the danger of death awaits her.

Clara is seriously affected by this incident and ponders over it long. Since she accepts the evidence of her senses when she knows she is fully awake, she considers the warning to have been a valid one, but she and the reader later learn that it was merely Carwin trying to frighten her away from the summerhouse, where he is carrying on an affair with her servant, Judith. She dismisses the dream, on the other hand, as purely imaginary, as a mere phantom (1:86), when in reality it forewarns her of a danger that does indeed impend. The rationalist in Clara, however, does not accept the dream as anything but a fantasy, and she finds it impossible to explain the ideas that subsequently well up in her mind. The following month, after Pleyel, whom she loves, has failed to appear for an appointed rehearsal of a new German play, she fears some accident may have befallen him, and she sits in her room that night musing upon the dangers and cares of human life. Recalling by association, then, her father's terrible end, she decides to read in the memoirs of his life that he had left in manuscript. She starts to her closet to get it, unaware that Carwin is trapped inside, but remembering the whispered voices she had heard coming from that room a number of weeks before, she is suddenly filled with fear. Her mind darts to the conclusion that some being with evil intent lies concealed within (1:84).

Since all these events take place in enclosures that have special significance for Clara, they must be interpreted as symbols of her mind. The summerhouse, enclosed with both lattice and vines, lies in a deeply secluded recess that can be reached only by a "rugged and intricate" path (1:63). Like the temple, it is a place of isolation and introspection that suggests her mental state. So too is her dwelling, separated as it is from the main house of her family by a quarter of a mile. Within is her room, where a number of strange and frightening events occur, and appended to it is her closet, which seems to represent the inner recesses of her mind. Here, most significantly, she keeps her father's manuscript. In each of these enclosures, Clara becomes the victim of strange mental processes: the prophetic dream that occurs in the summerhouse, and her infatuation with Carwin's picture and the feeling of anguish for her brother and his children that comes to her mind while alone in her room. With these events in mind, the reader is prepared for the series of powerful mental shocks that Clara receives when she turns to her closet to retrieve her father's manuscript.

Clara is unable to account for the mental process that follows. Her faith in the validity of her sensations is shaken when, hearing a voice that seems to come from behind her and that warns her away from the door, she looks about the room but sees nothing. "Which of my senses," she asks, "was the prey of a fatal illusion?" (1:85). That she heard the sound cannot be doubted, yet the person who seemed to be standing at her right ear when he spoke is nowhere to be seen. She begins to wonder, too, at the strange parallel between this experience and her frightening dream in the summerhouse. On the night of her dream, she was made aware "by some inexplicable contrivance" of the danger that impended. Yet, she writes, "my actions and sensations were those of one wholly unacquainted with it. Now, was it not equally true that my actions and persuasions were at war? Had not the belief, that evil lurked in the closet, gained admittance, and had not my actions betokened an unwarrantable security?" (1:86–87). Clara is deeply disturbed by the strange relation that seems to exist between the danger she perceives and the way she reacts when she learns of it and by the similar voices that have warned her of her peril.

As she ponders the problem, moreover, Clara arrives at a conclusion that, although unsupported by any reasonable evidence and wrong in the immediate incident, is nonetheless essentially right in pinpointing both the person she should fear and the danger that threatens. Since the voice that warns her away from the closet recalls the one that saved her in her dream, and since it saved her then from her brother, who seemed to beckon her to destruction, she becomes convinced that it is Wieland who lurks in the closet and that he intends to kill her. Clara struggles against this idea as a "strange and terrible chimera," but it will not be dismissed. She concludes, therefore, that "it was surely no vulgar agency that gave this form to [her] fears. He to whom all parts of time are equally present, whom no contingency approaches, was the author of that spell which now seized upon [her]." Yet even though she believes that an omen of her fate has been communicated to her in her dream, she cannot understand why she does not flee the evil that approaches. Indeed, she actually rushes to meet it, for in her strange infatuation, she tries to force the closet door and calls on him within to come out. It is small wonder, then, that Clara concludes from her experience: "Ideas exist in our minds that can be accounted for by no established laws" (1:87).

That Brown expects the reader to entertain this conclusion seriously is apparent from the ensuing action, because he makes no attempt to explain away Clara's dream or the strange thoughts and actions that follow it. Subsequent events, in fact, only confirm her prophetic fears, for once Wieland has killed his wife and children, his imagined voices demand the death of Clara as well; and three times escaping from prison to pursue her, he makes several violent attempts on her life. When Clara finally learns, moreover, that Wieland in his madness has sought to kill her, she recalls her dream. "I recollected the omens of this destiny," she writes; "I remembered the gulf to which my brother's invitation had conducted me; I remembered that, when on the brink of danger, the author of my peril was depicted by my fears in his form: Thus realized, were the creatures of prophetic sleep, and of wakeful terror" (1:189–90). Indeed, the dream is prophetic in yet another sense. When Wieland is on the point of killing her at the climax of the book, he is stopped by the same voice, Carwin's, and by the same command that had saved her in the dream (1:229).

Clara is almost destroyed by all that happens, for the very foundations of her life have been swept away from her. She comes to question the validity of her sensations and to doubt her ability to act in accordance with their promptings. Her mind leaps to conclusions for which there is no sensory evidence, but subsequent events confirm their truth. She finds herself reviled by Pleyel on the basis of valid if misinterpreted sensations, and she sees her brother fall victim to an inherited mania that makes him a prey to illusory sense impressions. Her mind is unstrung at the deaths of Catharine and the children, and after her final encounter with the maniacal Wieland, she goes completely mad and retreats into the room where the terrifying experience overwhelmed her. In refusing to leave her chambers, she dwells in isolation on the calamities that have befallen her. One night, however, while she dreams a fantastic dream that reveals the turbulence of her mental state, the house catches fire and, after her rescue, burns to the ground. Clara is forced to return to the world. Taken to Europe by her rationalist uncle, she eventually marries Pleyel, whom Carwin has disabused of his errors, and finally regains her mental equilibrium.

This happy solution to Clara's problems—appended as a final chapter that Brown probably wrote just before the book was published—is not at all satisfactory. It obscures the more serious conclusion toward which the action of the novel had been tending: that human beings are much more complex than contemporary psychology assumed and that their motives and actions are not so easily explained.[15] To be sure, the burning of Clara's house is a nice touch since at one stroke it cuts her off from her past. But Clara has had a traumatic experience. She has discovered mysterious aspects of herself for which she cannot account, and she suffers from anxieties and fears that seem to have no rational cause but turn out to be prophetic. She receives a severe shock in her brother's maniacal behavior and so far refuses to accept the fact that he is guilty of his crimes that she persists in believing that Carwin is the direct cause of his acts. So distraught has she been, in other words, that her recovery as the result of a change of scene, the care of her rationalist uncle, and her marriage to Pleyel does not ring true.

Carwin

Yet another variation on the theme of the book is presented through Carwin, the strange young man who precipitates the action by rashly using his power of ventriloquism. Carwin presents a problem that the other characters cannot solve. He seems at first to be only a country bumpkin, but once they get to know him, they discover that he is a man of great intellect, vast knowledge, and a high degree of skill in communicating it to others (1:72, 76). Pleyel, who had met him three years before in Spain, believes that he is English by birth and a Roman Catholic, and he and the Wielands find it difficult to reconcile the various impressions they have of him. Although they are curious to learn what he is doing in America, Carwin is secretive and gives them no clue to his past. He has, of course, violated their minds by projecting the voices in the temple, the summerhouse, and Clara's bedroom and closet, but when they mention the strange events to him, he gives them a rational explanation that is very close to the truth: the mysterious voices came from a human agent skilled in mimicry.

That they cannot explain the motives of one who would act so strangely, he tells them, is of no consequence, for we never fully know "the condition and designs of" those who surround us (1:75–76). Carwin is telling the literal truth. The Wielands and Pleyel cannot hope to penetrate the facade he presents, and they even become the dupes of a deception when they believe a report that he is a murderer and escaped prisoner. Readers of *Wieland* are equally in the dark until they read *Memoirs of Carwin the Biloquist,* a fragment that was not published in conjunction with *Wieland* until the twentieth century.[16] Here we learn that Carwin, an American youth, had come under the influence of a man named Ludloe, whose faith in the idea of progress and human perfectibility had turned him into a utopian planner. Ludloe hoped to recruit Carwin into a secret society, and under his tutorship the young man became fired with the belief that a few "enlightened and disinterested" men might establish an ideal state with "a new race" who would eventually "overflow the habitable world" (1:277–78).

Since Carwin's memoir is only a fragment, we do not know his entire story. The reason for his break with Ludloe and flight to America is only hinted at, but enough has been written to make it clear that Carwin had become enamored of radical thought. A man of great curiosity, his thirst for knowledge had been insatiable, but his education, unguided by any firm moral principle, had been left to his own initiative and understanding. Hence, even before he meets Ludloe, Carwin is capable of fallacious reasoning by which he tries to argue that the ends he seeks justify the means he will use to attain them, an error that is only confirmed by his master. He comes to believe, finally, that his duty may sometimes require him to use imposture and that his own best interest may be served by the sacrifice of truth (1:273–74, 285–86). In short, despite his excellent mind and vast knowledge, the way is opened for Carwin to act as his own passions and desires prompt him yet to justify those actions to himself by fallacious reasoning. His experience in *Wieland,* therefore, illustrates the errors into which the radical thinker can fall and the evil consequences that may ensue.

Carwin's errors, moreover, become progressively worse as the action of *Wieland* develops. Trapped in the temple by the approach of Wieland, Carwin first uses his power of ventriloquism to extricate himself, believing that his own safety demands his concealment. On the second occasion, thinking that no "inconvenience could possibly have flowed from" the first, he breaks into the conversation between Wieland and Pleyel, and he deceives himself with the thought that he is actually "conferring a benefit on all parties" concerned (1:200). In each case, he justifies the imposture by convincing himself that it is harmless or that he is achieving a benevolent end. It soon becomes apparent, however, that, once having used his power, he takes pleasure—as he later tells Clara—in the mystery he creates (1:201), and his motives, never pure or untinged with selfishness, increasingly darken as he continues to act. In menacing Clara in her room late at night, he is frankly trying to satisfy the cravings of his abnormal curiosity without regard for the rights of another, and in trying to frighten her from the summerhouse, he is seeking to maintain a trysting place where he can satisfy his lecherous desires with Judith. Indeed, he even performs a truly monstrous act when he gleefully deludes Pleyel by deliberately blasting Clara's reputation.

Though Carwin may argue the absence of malignant intent in extenuation of his deeds, perceptive readers see that he is really a creature almost totally without heart who thinks first of himself and who obviously enjoys the power he can exert over other, less knowing people. More important, he is willing to interfere in the lives of others with his imposture, despite the fact he can never know what chain reaction he may set in motion. Thus, although he maintains to the end that he meditated no harm against the Wielands, by using his power of ventriloquism to escape from the temple, he initiates a series of events that ends only with the deaths of Catharine and the children and with Wieland's suicide. To be sure, when Carwin meets the Wielands some time after he first projects the voices, he tries to explain away the mystery by suggesting the truth, that a physical explanation for them is possible (1:75). But once having opened the mind of Wieland, however unintentionally, to the possibility of his having received direct communication from the deity, he can never foresee or control the result that follows. One can never predict the reactions of another, as Carwin learns in his experience with Clara, who does not always act as expected when she hears the mysterious voices.

The career of Carwin, therefore, seems to suggest the dangers that lie in the path of one who attempts to lead his life according to rationalist principles. A great accumulation of knowledge of human affairs does not enable one to foresee with any certainty the consequences of one's acts—nor can one always estimate justly one's own motivations. Though Carwin resembles Pleyel in his demand for rationalistic explanations of unusual phenomena (1:75) and is a man of great intellectual ability, he nonetheless falls easy prey to fallacious reasoning and is incapable of resisting the temptation to use his power, even when he knows he should not. A rather cold and heartless villain, he is impelled by selfish motives and is all too willing to meddle egotistically in the affairs of others. Hence, it seems fair to conclude that in the character of Carwin, Brown casts serious doubts on the ability of even exceptional human beings to overcome their basic human imperfections or to create a new society where the woes of the present world will be corrected. Indeed, Brown seems to imply that such utopian planners, left to the guidance of their own understanding, are likely to do more harm than good.

Read in these terms, *Wieland* is clearly a much more important intellectual document than much of the criticism would have us believe. It is certainly not merely the attack on religious fanaticism or the open exposition of rationalist principles that some of the critics have contended.[17] In fact, one might more reasonably conclude that the absence of proper moral and religious teaching contributes at least as much to the destruction of the Wieland circle as any other factor. To be sure, Clara informs the reader in the first paragraph of the book that the tale "will exemplify the force of early impressions," and this statement must be taken to mean the baleful influence of the elder Wieland's mysterious death. But Clara goes on to say that it is also intended to show "the immeasurable evils that flow from an erroneous or imperfect discipline" (1:5), a concept that can certainly be applied to Carwin's training at the hands of Ludloe and to Clara and Theodore Wieland's education. Clara is quite explicit on the point that their education was influenced by no religious standard, that they were left entirely "to the guidance of [their] own understanding, and the casual impressions" of society (1:22). Such a passage certainly invites the interpretation that the absence of religious training was a serious fault in their education.[18]

This is not to say that the book affirms a system of moral or religious value. It does not. A serious weakness in the novel is that possible alternatives to the view that Brown consistently questions are left so disturbingly vague, that no true source for them is even suggested. Thus, in the conclusion, when Clara moralizes on the events of the story, she observes that all the victimized characters, through their errors and frailty, contributed to some extent to their own destruction. And she writes: "If Wieland had framed juster notions of moral duty, and of the divine attributes; or if I had been gifted with ordinary equanimity or foresight, the double-tongued deceiver would have been baffled and repelled" (1:244). Such a conclusion, however, will not do. It does not take into account the sources of error that afflict both Pleyel and Carwin, and it fails to provide any system of value in terms of which the characters could have corrected their errors and acted more wisely than they did. *Wieland* must therefore be considered an intellectually truncated book, the greatest importance of which lies not in the moralized conclusion but in its systematic questioning of some fundamental tenets of the Enlightenment.

Literary Value and Importance

Indeed, it is this probing quality of *Wieland* that reveals most clearly the book's historical value, for elements in the novel reecho down the century in a number of different writers. Larzer Ziff has already observed that the theme he perceives in *Wieland* appears again in the works of Hawthorne and Melville,[19] but other aspects of the book recur in later writers also. Certainly both James Fenimore Cooper and Herman Melville were concerned with the problem of *Wieland,* for both, in some of their works, raised the question of whether human beings, through the use of their senses and reason alone, could arrive at a true understanding of the nature of reality. The question informs, among others, Cooper's final novel, *The Ways of the Hour,* which illustrates, through the use of a murder trial, the trouble people have in forming valid opinions on the basis of physical evidence, and it lies at the heart of Melville's "Benito Cereno," in which Amasa Delano fails utterly in arriving at a just interpretation of the reality that presents itself to his senses. Unlike Brown and Melville, of course, Cooper found his affirmative values in conservative Christian belief, but all three are alike in their interest in and aesthetic use of the fundamental question.

Other elements too recur in subsequent writers. The intellectual curiosity of Carwin that permits him to experiment on Clara to see if she is really so courageous as she seems (1:201–2) and that prompts him to invade her room and probe into her journal (1:205–6) clearly foreshadows the cold and sagacious intellectuality that appears in the heartless villains, like Ethan Brand and Roger Chillingworth, that Hawthorne was later to create. The isolation of the Wielands—their withdrawal from the society of others—and the symbols—farm, house, temple—through which it is expressed remind one somewhat of the thematic use of the concept in Hawthorne's fiction. Indeed, there is even a Jamesian element in *Wieland* when the characters attempt to read each other's motives and emotions, as in the incident in which Clara interprets the look on Pleyel's face to arrive at an awareness of what *his* interpretation of her motives and actions might be (1:115–16). Such sophistication of technique is by no means usual with Brown, and he makes no attempt to sustain it. Yet resemblances like these do reveal how much of later American fiction is foreshadowed in this novel.

Brown's use of the Gothic mode provides yet another means for estimating the significance of his book for later fiction. Adapting the devices he found in contemporary British and German novels to his own psychological purposes, he made the enclosures in *Wieland* symbols of his characters' minds and so projected their mental states into the external world that the space they inhabit and their mental states become one. The temple, the summerhouse, and Clara's room and closet derive from such enclosures as the castle, abbey, or catacombs found in the Gothic novel in Europe, but they are also the prototypes of a kind of enclosure that was to recur in American literature throughout the nineteenth century. They foreshadow such well-known symbols as, among others, Roderick Usher's house and Prince Prospero's suite of rooms in Poe's tales; Rappaccini's garden and Aylmer's laboratory in Hawthorne's fiction; or the house at Bly and the labyrinth of rooms through which Spencer Brydon searches for his other self in the stories of Henry James. In *Wieland,* Brown domesticated Gothic fiction and established for the ensuing century the symbolic vocabulary in terms of which the psychological Gothic tale would be developed.[20]

To insist on its historical importance, however, is to do the book a disservice, for *Wieland* is well worth reading today for its intrinsic value. Admittedly the book contains flaws. Like all of Brown's other novels, it is structurally weak, undoubtedly the result of the haste with which it was written. The Stuart-Conway subplot, introduced early, is soon dropped completely, and Brown brings his tale almost to the end without mentioning it further. He crowds the major part of it into the final chapter, where it appears as a kind of extraneous afterthought and throws the book off balance. Although he tries to integrate the material thematically into the book, he does not succeed. The now-recovered Clara takes up the subplot only after her own story has been completed and she has accounted for the subsequent career of Carwin. Then, at the very end, she tries to draw a parallel between the experience of the Wielands and that of the characters in the subplot. The attempt does not work. We are left instead with a contrived ending, one that distorts to a considerable degree both the form and the meaning of the book.

Occasionally the language of *Wieland* also leaves much to be desired. The latinate words and involved circumlocutions, which several critics have noted,[21] must be considered flaws, especially when they appear in contexts where the effect can only be described as ludicrous. A few extreme examples will illustrate the fault. In a passage that rather successfully creates a feeling of suspense as Clara listens for whispers in her room late at night, she unfortunately writes: "My habitation was a wooden edifice" (1:56). Much of the dramatic effect, for the moment, dissolves. Equally serious lapses occur elsewhere in the book. On the night of her father's strange death, her uncle hears a loud explosion and dreadful shriek coming from the temple. "The incident was inexplicable," Clara writes, "but he could not fail to perceive the propriety of hastening to the spot" (1:17). In a similar fashion, her utter fright when murderers seem to be lurking in her closet evokes the expression: "Flight instantly suggested itself as most eligible in circumstances so perilous" (1:58). Not all of the stylistic faults, of course, are so serious as these, yet one would like to wish them away from a book that has so many really fine qualities to recommend it.

Errors in structure and style aside, there is much to be said for the skill with which Brown developed the novel. The central part of the story is, in fact, rather well constructed. Between the introduction of the subplot in chapter 4 and the regrettable conclusion, the main plot proceeds at a steady pace, all parts subordinated to the central theme, and moving with a powerful force. Brown's use of his characters to illustrate different temperaments reacting in several ways to a series of odd phenomena was a happy invention. It provided the variety he needed in the development of his theme, yet at the same time it enabled him to maintain a central unity in terms of the related meanings expressed or implied through their varied experiences. The action, moreover, moves forward with scarcely a check, each incident developing out of the one that went before with a kind of inexorable force that suggests the lack of control human beings have over the events they set in motion. The fate of the characters is thus made to appear the logical result of the way they react to external pressures in the kind of world that Brown chooses to posit.

The style of the novel, moreover, despite the serious lapses, fits rather well this mode of development. The short, staccato sentences, reminiscent of parts of *Caleb Williams,*[22] move the tale forward in a kind of breathless fashion and are, for the most part, perfectly appropriate to the narrator. In the first chapter of the book, Clara sets the tone for much of what is to follow: "My state is not destitute of tranquillity. The sentiment that dictates my feelings is not hope. Futurity has no power over my thoughts. To all that is to come I am perfectly indifferent. With regard to myself, I have nothing more to fear. Fate has done its worst. Henceforth, I am callous to misfortune" (1:5). The movement of these sentences reflects the emotional state of the speaker, and the reader is prepared to accept the paragraph as the proper expression for the obviously distraught person who is telling the story. Brown, of course, does not always maintain this pitch. Indeed, he could not without soon wearying the reader. Hence, when Clara tells of her father's background or describes their pleasant idyllic life before any voices are heard, her sentences lengthen considerably and become calmer in tone. At moments of stress, on the other hand, and most especially when she breaks under the emotional strain of her experience, she approaches the somewhat nervous, but highly effective, tone of the quoted passage.

Most of the book's artistic success, however, derives from Brown's manipulation of the point of view, both in the parts that Clara reports herself and those in which she records the speeches of others. By his use of the first-person technique, Brown is able to create a great deal of suspense in that the reader has no more information at any time than does the character through whose eyes the story is told. The importance of this device is obvious enough in those episodes in which Clara is faced with danger, and the reader moves along excitedly to find out what will happen. Not all of the episodes, however, are developed at this simple level. The night of the father's death, for example, is largely described from the mother's point of view, and though the reader is thus removed several steps from the event, the distance rather adds than detracts from the reader's interest. Clara, a child of six at the time, has heard the tale from her uncle, and she repeats the story as he must have told it to her. Thus, Clara reveals what happened through a description of her mother's thoughts and actions, as her father, full of apprehension, waits for the stroke of midnight.

The means Brown uses in detailing the incident add greatly to its effect, for he carefully underplays the emotionalism implicit in the scene by describing only the physical manifestations of the characters' emotional states. We perceive the elder Wieland's terror as his wife apprehended it, through his "frequent and anxious glances" at the clock as the hands approach midnight, through the visible shock to his frame as the hour tolls, and through the trembling of his joints that makes it difficult for him to throw on a loose gown. When he goes to the rock, the focus shifts to the mother, and we perceive her emotional state in the same way. Her anxiety drives her from her bed: "She rose, and seated herself at the window. She strained her sight to get a view of the dome, and of the path that led to it." There she sits, anxiously trying to pierce the darkness, when, half an hour later, a light, an explosion, and her husband's shrieks announce the catastrophe (1:15–16). By describing the scene in this way, Brown maintains both a physical and psychological distance from the event. He makes the remarkable death of the father artistically acceptable and manages to suggest, at the same time, the sense of awe and mystery with which Clara and Wieland naturally look back on the most important event of their childhood.

More important, however, in terms of both structure and meaning is Brown's use of point of view to serve a thematic purpose in the book.[23] Since the story is told through the person of Clara, we see the various events of the novel as they appear to her, and we follow her line of reasoning as she tries to interpret them. But on three occasions, Clara is forced to confront another's account of what has happened, and in each case the shift in point of view brings both Clara and the reader enlightenment. The first occurs when Pleyel accuses her of being Carwin's mistress, an accusation all the more startling because she fully perceives for the first time the fantastic errors that one can fall into by simply misinterpreting true sensations. Both she and the reader know, for example, that she has acted prudently on the night she confronts Carwin in her room, but Pleyel's speech clearly shows how seriously he has misinterpreted each of the actions that she innocently performed. It also reveals, moreover, how plausible is his interpretation of the events—once his mind has been disposed to believe in her infamy.

An even more startling enlightenment comes after Catharine's death, for it does not occur to Clara at first that Wieland has killed her. Instead, when Wieland approaches her after the event, she misreads both his appearance and his actions: first, as indicating that he has not yet learned of his wife's death (1:152); and, second, that he has, and has gone mad with anguish (1:153–54). When the approach of others makes him turn from her and flee, Clara becomes so distraught that she is hardly aware of what is going on around her. She goes completely mad when she learns of the children's deaths too, and after her recovery, she arrives at the conclusion—"an unavoidable inference," she calls it (1:161)—that Carwin is guilty of the crimes. Clara is ripe for her second shock, which comes when she reads Wieland's defense of himself before the court that convicts him—a remarkable document that connotes quite well the madness of his belief that he has acted righteously in destroying his family. Clara is forced to admit, therefore, that Carwin did not actually commit the crimes, but resisting to the end the belief that Wieland is truly guilty, she insists that Carwin must surely have been the evil influence behind them.

It remains, then, only for Carwin's story to be finally told and the extent of his guilt established for Clara to perceive the web of misunderstanding and misinterpretation in which she has been caught. Meeting Carwin at last in her house, she hears him explain the mystery of the voices all have heard yet firmly maintain his innocence concerning those that commanded Wieland to kill. At this point Clara hardly knows what to believe. Events come rapidly to a climax, however, with the appearance of Wieland; his attempt on Clara's life, which is thwarted by Carwin; and his ultimate suicide when he learns that he has been the victim of his own illusory sensations. Clara's mind breaks under the strain almost as if it were shattered at perceiving the truth of what has happened, a truth that could not be finally established without the self-revelatory speeches of the other characters. The shifted point of view thus provides the fundamental contrast between events as they are and events as the characters see them that lies at the thematic heart of the novel.

Brown is by no means so successful as more recent writers have been in integrating all four points of view into a tightly knit whole. There is a certain awkwardness in the way the three speeches are introduced, and they are not all equally satisfactory in the handling. In fact, Wieland's address to the court is by far the best. One could wish too that more of Carwin's background had been introduced into his speech—rather than in the *Memoirs* fragment—so that one might gain a fuller insight into his character without going beyond the limits of the novel itself. To overemphasize these weaknesses, however, would be to miss the point of Brown's remarkable achievement, for *Wieland* is a fascinating book: it is intellectually interesting for its serious questioning of some of the tenets of eighteenth-century thought and aesthetically important for the form in which the theme found its expression. With all of its faults of structure and style, therefore, *Wieland* may well be considered a significant novel in its own right—as well as an important document in the history of American fiction.

Chapter Three
Ormond

Before *Wieland* was through the press, Charles Brockden Brown was already at work on another book, *Memoirs of Carwin the Biloquist,* to recount the early life of Carwin and describe his education at the hands of Ludloe. Elihu Hubbard Smith read part of the fragment as early as 8 August 1798, but on 4 September Brown wrote William Dunlap that he had abandoned the project "for the present."[1] The work was not published until Brown issued it serially in his *Literary Magazine and American Register* beginning in November 1803. Though he apparently worked on the story again in 1804–5,[2] the book was never finished, and it remains important in Brown's career largely because of its relation to *Wieland.* Narrated by Carwin himself, the book presents his background and youth, the discovery of his amazing power, and his attempts to justify to himself the use of it for personal ends. He is taken up by Ludloe, a utopian planner, who recruits him for his secret purposes but demands that he first reveal everything about himself. The narrative breaks off just as Carwin resolves not to tell Ludloe of his biloquial powers, a decision that presumably leads to a break with Ludloe and the persecution of Carwin hinted at in *Wieland.*

When Brown laid aside the unfinished *Memoirs of Carwin,* he turned at once to another tale, *Memoirs of Stephen Calvert,* which Smith reports he was reading on 4 September.[3] The outbreak of yellow fever, however, soon put an end to Brown's writing. Smith died on 19 September, and Brown soon left New York to visit Dunlap in Perth Amboy, where he hoped to recuperate from the illness he too had contracted. Brown arrived on 24 September, and the following day Dunlap recorded in his diary that he was reading *Stephen Calvert.*[4] Brown remained with Dunlap for nearly a month, leaving on 21 October for Burlington, and, eventually, Philadelphia. Back in New York in mid-November, he was soon at work on yet another book. He had bargained with Hocquet Caritat, the publisher of *Wieland,* to complete a new novel, *Ormond,* only part of which had been written. Printing began at once, and, as Brown wrote his brother Armitt in December 1798, he had to apply himself diligently to the writing "in order to keep pace with the press." So absorbed was he in his work that he was scarcely aware of the passage of time, and he finished each day's task "thoroughly weary" and quite unfit for even writing a letter.[5]

In composing *Ormond,* perhaps the most intellectual of his novels, Brown drew heavily on his reading. In form, the book derives from the British tale of seduction made popular by Samuel Richardson, and it includes some Gothic elements as well. But as Brown developed his novel, he used material from many sources. To Ormond, he gave opinions drawn directly, as Sydney J. Krause has shown, from William Godwin's *Political Justice,*[6] and he made the character a utopian projector and member of a secret organization, much like the subversive Society of the Illuminati, a group of "Perfectibilists" that existed briefly in eighteenth-century Europe, and which had recently been treated in such works as John Robison's *Proofs of a Conspiracy against All the Religions and Governments of Europe* (1797), the translator's note appended to Friedrich von Schiller's *The Ghost-Seer* (1795), and even a novel, Karl Grosse's *Horrid Mysteries* (1797).[7] Brown included as well many references to recent events in both America and Europe, especially the French Revolution,[8] and although he certainly wrote very rapidly, he managed to create a rich historical background for the action and to maintain a reasonably consistent chronology of events. He completed the writing around New Year's Day, and the book was published in January 1799.[9]

A Feminist Novel

Ormond; or, The Secret Witness, a strongly feminist book, is told in the first person by Sophia Westwyn Courtland, who plays no important role in the action until rather late in the novel. Sophia recounts the life of her friend, Constantia Dudley,[10] an intelligent young lady who exhibits the virtues of constancy and fortitude, who chooses to remain single rather than to contract what she deems are unsuitable marriages, and who makes her way in the world by using her own good sense. Indeed, Constantia Dudley may well be considered the living embodiment of some of the principles Brown had aired in the first two parts of *Alcuin,*[11] and the whole action of the novel well illustrates Brown's attitude toward the rights of women: their need for a sounder education, their right to be treated as free individuals, and their ability, once properly trained, to act in the practical world. An even more radical idea, expressed in the unpublished sections of *Alcuin,* also appears in the book in Ormond's opposition, despite some vacillation on his part, to the institution of marriage, but his position, unlike that put forth in

Alcuin, derives from the low opinion that, until he meets Constantia, he has of women.

Other elements too remind readers of Brown's previous work. The theme of deceptive appearance occurs as it did in *Wieland,* embodied in *Ormond* in the characters of Thomas Craig and Ormond, both of whom cause great trouble for the Dudley family. The excellent presence and plausible story of Craig—in whose "open and ingenuous aspect" few could fail to place confidence (2:99)—allow him to gain the trust of Stephen Dudley, Constantia's father. Craig seems to be all that one could desire, first as an apprentice in Dudley's business and later as a partner, but his true nature is finally revealed by the act of embezzlement that plunges the Dudley family into ruin and triggers the main action of the story. So too does Ormond, the principal villain of the piece, hide his real character behind the mask of apparent frankness and candor to lead Constantia, at the end of the novel, to the very brink of disaster. The truth is almost as hard to discern behind the appearance of things as it was in *Wieland,* and the characters make some serious mistakes in their judgment of men and their motives.

In characterization, too, *Ormond* resembles the books on which Brown had recently been working. Ormond, for example—the proud, intelligent, artful villain—is closely related to both Ludloe and Carwin. All three are—or have been—proponents of contemporary radical thought, and all are willing to use unscrupulous means to achieve what they believe are beneficent ends. Ormond and Ludloe are especially alike in that each is a member of a secret revolutionary organization. The purposes of these men are only hinted at, but they seem desirous of remaking the world according to utopian principles, and to this end they have set up ideal commonwealths in some remote part of the world. Ludloe's seems to be on the northeast coast of Australia (1:299), Ormond's on either "the shore of an *Austral* continent, or in the heart of desert America" (2:252). Although Carwin, Ludloe, and Ormond differ in certain specific attributes and talents, all three clearly illustrate the dangerous extremes to which contemporary revolutionary thought could lead the unrestrained thinker. Indeed, Carwin and Ormond, in particular, cause serious trouble to others in giving free rein to their wills.

Even the heroines of *Ormond* and *Wieland* bear a certain, though perhaps only superficial, resemblance to each other. Each is an attractive and "enlightened" young lady whose life and happiness are threatened by the duplicity of the villain. Constantia Dudley, a carefully reared girl of sixteen, has, like Clara Wieland, been given an education that raises her above the general intellectual level of her sex. Instead of providing her merely with the genteel feminine accomplishments of music and art, Constantia's father "conducted her to the school of Newton and Hartley, unveiled to her the mathematical properties of light and sound, taught her as a metaphysician and anatomist, the structure and power of the senses, and discussed with her the principles and progress of human society" (2:33). Unlike Clara, Constantia does not live apart from the world. Instead, Brown deliberately thrusts her into the mainstream of life where she meets and survives a series of physical troubles before Ormond even appears on the scene. Her encounter with Ormond, when it finally does occur in the latter half of the book, is also more direct and personal than Clara's had been with Carwin, and Constantia's total experience has, on the whole, a far more positive meaning than Clara's has in *Wieland.*

Constantia Dudley is by far the stronger woman, and the many experiences she goes through are designed to illustrate the constancy and fortitude of her character. After Thomas Craig's embezzlement of her father's funds—a crime made possible by Stephen Dudley's desire for increased wealth and leisure, which leads him to entrust the entire business to his young partner—Constantia's mother dies, and the girl is forced to assume the whole burden of the household when her father first succumbs to drunkenness and then goes blind. Constantia rises to the occasion, but her struggle is a difficult one. The practical knowledge she acquires is painfully learned, for tasks that "to age and experience" would not have been difficult are very arduous to her. She overcomes her initial reluctance to act and executes her duties "with address and dispatch. One, marking her deportment, would have perceived nothing but dignity and courage. He would have regarded these as the fruits of habitual independence and exertion, whereas they were merely the results of clear perceptions and inflexible resolves" (2:31).

Brown does not present his heroine as an impossible ideal. Indeed, her friend Sophia goes out of her way to insist upon her defects (2:3) and clearly states that Constantia, like the general mass of men, judged "from the most obvious appearances, and was subject like them to impulses which distained the controul of her reason" (2:42). Though her motives are generally pure, Constantia does not escape the common lot of men, whose decisions are seldom, if ever, "totally uninfluenced by sinister and selfish motives." Indeed, at one point in the novel, her thoughts are swayed by a bias in favor of Ormond, though she herself is completely unaware that they are (2:157). Nonetheless, as long as Constantia's problem is purely one of survival in a dangerous—indeed, at times, even hostile—world, her decisions are rationally made and adhered to with fortitude and courage. Thus, when left alone to care for her blind father and a dependent servant girl, Constantia acts decisively. She finds suitable quarters for them to live in, learns how to sew for a living, and, when the yellow fever epidemic reduces her income to practically nothing, manages to survive the plague by buying three bushels of Indian meal and salt—enough to sustain the three of them for four months (2:56–57). Through her foresight, the Dudleys are able to live though the prices of food rise and no work is to be had.

Constantia, moreover, attempts to fulfill her human obligations to the best of her understanding and ability. When her neighbor, Mary Whiston, comes down with the yellow fever, Constantia goes to her, and, at considerable personal danger, she tries to help the girl, whose brother, out of fear for his own life, has deserted her and fled to the country. Despite all that Constantia can do, Mary dies of the disease. Although on the point of collapse herself, she perseveres to the end and sees that Mary's corpse is properly disposed of. Constantia eventually contracts the disease, but no sooner is she up and around again than she visits an old neighbor, Sarah Baxter, whose husband is dying, takes over from the distraught widow, and sets the house aright again. In other human relations, Constantia is equally noble. When, after the plague has subsided, she runs into Thomas Craig, she forgives the wrong he has done her father, lays aside all thoughts of prosecution, and simply asks that he give her some money to relieve her distress. Brown has obviously developed his tale to this point as a kind of modern virtue story,[12] the theme of which seems to be the value of the sort of education that enables a woman to live and act in the practical world.

Such a conclusion is certainly supported by the variations that Brown rings upon the theme, for he introduces two other female characters who go through similar experiences but who stand in strong contrast to Constantia.[13] They are Helena Cleves, Ormond's mistress, whose education has made her fit to be little more than the plaything of men, and Martinette de Beauvais, who turns out to be Ormond's sister, a woman whose freedom and worldly experience have all but unsexed her. Like Constantia Dudley, each has been thrown upon her own resources in the world, for Helena's father dies suddenly and leaves her penniless, and Martinette has been on her own from the time when, as a young girl in Europe, she lost both parents and her foster father disappeared on a trip to the West Indies. Since all three have been placed abruptly in similar circumstances, the way they react to their misfortunes reveals the relative worth of the principles by which they live. Neither Helena Cleves nor Martinette de Beauvais solves her problem so well as does Constantia Dudley. Indeed, both fail miserably.

Like most others of her sex, Helena Cleves had been given only a superficial education, one that made her an accomplished musician and a sprightly conversationalist but did not prepare her "to sustain [the] reverse of fortune, in a graceful manner" (2:121). She has never been trained to think beyond the day but has simply eaten and drunk what others have provided. Indeed, as Constantia clearly recognizes, Helena is as "ignorant and helpless as a child, on every topic that relates to the procuring of subsistence," for "her education [had] disabled her from standing alone" (2:141). A creature of the senses who can arouse little more than an emotional response in others, Helena falls easy prey to the seductions of Ormond, who, strongly opposed to marriage, takes her as his mistress despite the fact that she is obviously his intellectual inferior. When the more intelligent Constantia crosses his path, however, he casts his mistress aside, and Helena, devoid of inner resources and unable to bear the shock of this betrayal, can find no solution to her problem but suicide. Thus, in the character of Helena Cleves, one of the best-drawn minor characters in the book, Brown attacks the type of education that makes a woman utterly incapable of withstanding the vicissitudes of life.

At the other extreme is Martinette de Beauvais, a woman whose education has, like Constantia's, enabled her to survive but who places no limits upon what she will attempt to do. A devotee of revolt and liberty, she has played an active role in the bloodbath of the French Revolution and has competed with men in the most masculine of occupations, that of a soldier. If Helena Cleves is wrong in being so dependent upon others, Martinette errs in the other direction by seeking to be completely unrestrained. Constantia recognizes the French woman's error. Although she is at first attracted to Martinette because she believes she sees a likeness to herself in her strange acquaintance, she soon develops an antipathy to her when she learns of the atrocious acts that Martinette can justify to herself in the name of liberty. Constantia listens greedily to all that Martinette has to say, but "not with approbation," and, although she seeks to learn more of Martinette's past and the deeds that other women performed during the Revolution, she feels dislike replacing her first affection for the melodramatic French woman (2:207–8)

The Major Conflict

Constantia Dudley thus occupies a middle ground between these extremes of female behavior. She is far superior to both of her friends in that she has learned to live independently in the practical world without destroying her moral sense in the process. Her success, however, is not complete. She has one deficiency that is not revealed until she survives her physical trials and faces an intellectual and moral one. Up to this point, Brown seems to say, her education has been sufficient to ensure her physical survival, but against the insidious influence of fallacious reasoning and seductive argument, she has not been properly fortified. "She was unguarded," Sophia informs us, "in a point, where, if not her whole, yet, doubtless, her principal security and strongest bulwark would have existed. She was unacquainted with religion. She was unhabituated to conform herself to any standard, but that connected with the present life. Matrimonial, as well as every other human duty, was disconnected in her mind, with any awful or divine sanction. She formed her estimate of good and evil, on nothing but terestrial and visible consequences" (2:179).

Constantia's weakness derives from a serious fault in her education. Her father, though himself a religious man, had conceived the idea that religious truth could not be taught through "infantile and premature instruction." He strove, therefore, to lead his little daughter's thoughts away from religious subjects with the result that, once she is grown, she comes to view religion "with absolute indifference." It is not that she is opposed to religious belief but that "her modes of study and reflection" had simply unfitted her for discussions of the subject; "her mind was seldom called to meditate" upon it; and, when it did occur, "her perceptions were vague and obscure" (2:179–80). Constantia has enough of a moral sense to be repulsed by Martinette's revelations, and she has, by and large, acted well when confronted by problems of conduct in the everyday world. But when she is faced with the moral and intellectual challenge of Ormond, to whom she is attracted but who seeks to make her his mistress, she falls into serious danger.

Her first encounter with Ormond is innocent enough. Perceiving that Helena Cleves is unhappy as his mistress, Constantia tries to persuade him to marry the girl and even attempts to change his course of action "by the change of his principles" (2:146). In coming to Helena's aid, however, Constantia engages in debate with an adversary she is hardly prepared to meet and who uses unscrupulous means to attain his desires. Constantia, moreover, unwittingly places herself in a vulnerable position, for as they discuss the question, Ormond perceives her obvious superiority to other women and is soon enamored of her. Indeed, the more forcefully she argues on Helena's behalf, the more convinced he becomes that he can be satisfied with no other woman than her. After the rejection and death of the unfortunate Helena, therefore, he determines to win Constantia by any means. To be sure, "if other terms were rejected, he was willing, for the sake of this good, to accept her as a wife; but this was a choice to be made, only when every expedient was exhausted, for reconciling her to a compact of a different kind." He pretends, however, to be frank in his treatment of her, challenges her to refute his antimarriage principles and even promises her "a candid audience and profound consideration to her arguments" (2:178–79).

What Constantia does not know is that despite the apparent candor of her adversary, he is not so open as he seems. Although by his own professions his claims to sincerity would appear to be unquestionable, he is actually a consummate actor who has made imposture a matter of principle. Years before he had frequently been the victim of the duplicity of others, and on one occasion, he had used his great talent for disguise and imitation to penetrate the false appearance of a man who had designs against him. Ormond professes to believe that he can protect himself from the machinations of other men only by such devices—that although he would like to be open and upright himself, the treachery of human beings compels him to use duplicity (2:115–16). Such are the fallacious reasons he uses to justify his acts, but Ormond is not merely the victim of self-deception. Like Carwin in *Wieland,* he enjoys the power his unusual talent gives him. "It enabled him to gain access, as if by supernatural means, to the privacy of others, and baffle their profoundest contrivances to hide themselves from his view. It flattered him with the possession of something like Omniscience" (2:116).

The desire for power is indeed a major force in Ormond's motivation. He "aspired to nothing more ardently than to hold the reins of opinion. To exercise absolute power over the conduct of others, not by constraining their limbs, or by exacting obedience to his authority, but in a way of which his subjects should be scarcely conscious. He desired that his guidance should controul their steps, but that his agency, when most effectual, should be least suspected" (2:177). In his dealings with others, therefore, he pretends to speak openly and frankly, to state impartially the issue to be decided, and to allow the other to make the decision. Yet Ormond's treatment of Helena and Constantia is by no means so rational and honest. He influences the weak Helena in ways that even he was not himself entirely aware of (2:123), and he conceals from Constantia the means he intends to use to influence her decision. He hopes to change her opinions concerning marriage "by subtilty and perseverance"; but should he fail, he is "determined to adopt a system of imposture. To assume the guise of a convert to her doctrines, and appear as devout as herself in his notions of the sanctity of marriage" (2:179).[14]

In pursuing his purpose with Constantia, therefore, Ormond is careful never to disclose too much about himself. He does not reveal completely the projects that he has afoot in the world, and though he seems to take Constantia into his confidence and to answer explicitly all the questions she asks him, his disclosures, although ostensibly candid, always contain an element of obscurity, so that Constantia must always ask again and receive yet another unsatisfactory answer. By this means, he succeeds in guiding her mind in the direction he wants it to take, keeps alive her curiosity without ever fully satisfying it, and leads her on to ever new conjectures and doubts (2:177). In a similar fashion, he is careful to conceal from her his fundamental philosophy, for he knows how much it would repel her. Though indifferent to religion herself, she would be likely to consider his views insane. He conceives the universe merely as "a series of events, connected by an undesigning and inscrutable necessity, and an assemblage of forms, to which no begining or end can be conceived" (2:180). He believes, moreover, that until "the principles of the social machine" are changed, human beings can accomplish little but evil in the world (2:112). Utterly lacking in faith in anything beyond this world, Ormond is violently antireligious. In him, "enthusiasm [had been] added to disbelief, and he not only dissented but abhorred" (2:180).

Constantia is completely incapable of defeating an adversary whom she does not fully understand and who will use any unscrupulous means to subvert her opinions. Indeed, without religious faith, she runs the serious risk of being herself converted to his views. But Constantia is unaware of her peril. She entertains the idea that their differences of opinion concerning marriage might in time be reconciled, and though she tries to protect herself from self-delusion regarding him, she delights in the lucid letters he sends her while he is away. She is not so foolish, however, as to rely completely on herself, for she discusses the matter with her father and listens to his advice. Strongly opposed to "the political and anti-theological tenets" he has privately discovered Ormond possesses (2:181–82), Stephen Dudley clearly recognizes that, although it might be possible in time to restore Ormond "to the guidance of truth," it will not be done through any power his daughter possesses. Conformity in belief, he knows, "would flow from their marriage, but this conformity was not to be expected from" Ormond (2:211). Constantia acknowledges the soundness of her father's reasonings and agrees to delay her ultimate decision concerning Ormond and to accompany her father to Europe.

These plans are no sooner made, however, than Dudley is murdered, and Constantia would be completely unguarded were she not fortuitously reunited with Sophia Westwyn Courtland, an old friend and the narrator of the tale, who serves as perhaps an even stronger bulwark than Constantia's father. Like most of the other women in the story, Sophia has been faced with the problem of making her way in the practical world. Deserted at birth by a profligate mother, she has been reared by the Dudleys from infancy to her seventeenth year, but when her mother, now gone mad, makes demands on her, Sophia accompanies her to Europe and cares for her until her death. Though she marries a man named Courtland in Europe, Sophia does not forget her old friends but leaves him temporarily and travels to America to search out the Dudleys, from whom she has received no news. When the women are reunited, Constantia receives a strong ally in her struggle with Ormond, for Sophia, whose name means wisdom,[15] provides the one important element that Constantia lacks: the religious belief that Constantia's education had denied her. Unlike Ormond, who sees only blind necessity at work in the universe, Sophia believes in "divine superintendence" and knows "that all physical and moral agents, are merely instrumental to the purpose that [God] wills" (2:224). Thus, Sophia and Ormond directly oppose each other in the struggle to influence Constantia.

Developed thus far, Brown's novel seems to be moving toward an inevitable intellectual climax. Constantia has been positioned between Sophia and Ormond, much as she had between Helena Cleves and Martinette de Beauvais, but she is no longer merely the observer of the others' conduct. She has become the prize for which the others contend. The reader is disappointed to find, therefore, that the conflict between Sophia and Ormond never occurs, that the battle for Constantia is won without a struggle. Because of the observations she has made on men and manners in Europe, Sophia is able to estimate the character of Ormond in its true light, and she perceives that her inexperienced friend "had allowed herself to wander into untried paths, and had hearkened to positions, pregnant with destruction and ignominy." Sophia takes her firmly in hand. She points out to Constantia "the enormous errors" of Ormond, convinces her of the danger she faces in prolonging her relation with so dangerous a man, and readily obtains her consent to accompany her immediately on a voyage to England (2:253). Sophia's victory is won with astonishing ease.

Even more curious is Ormond's withdrawal from the struggle. Ormond had left the city before the murder of Stephen Dudley, so that he is absent when the women are reunited. When he does return, he makes no further attempt to persuade Constantia to his view. Instead, he informs her that he already knows her final decision concerning him, a revelation that startles Constantia since it was made in secret conversations with Sophia and has been communicated to no one. Only later does she learn that Ormond gained access to her house through a secret passage and eavesdropped on them from a hidden closet. He speaks enigmatically of an obstacle that still remains in his path, and he predicts that some unnamed disaster lies in her future. With this he leaves her, and we do not learn until later that Ormond has withdrawn from the struggle because, with the arrival of Sophia, he knew that he would not be able to penetrate the defenses that Constantia's scruples and the guidance of her friend would provide (2:281). The intellectual struggle for Constantia thus unexpectedly ended, Brown can do no more than conclude his tale with a scene of physical violence.

The events themselves can be quickly recounted. The women are separated when Constantia, leaving Philadelphia, visits a house she has acquired in New Jersey[16] while Sophia stays in New York to make the preparations for their journey. One evening just after sunset, Ormond appears at the house where Constantia, alone, is writing. He reveals that it was he who had driven Thomas Craig to murder her father and that he has just killed Craig himself. He insanely tries to argue that his motive was benevolent, that by the murder of her father he had conferred a benefit on her and would have ensured both her happiness and his had not Sophia appeared to bolster Constantia's defenses. Having abandoned all hope, therefore, of influencing her to accept him willingly as a lover, he intends to assault her at once. Constantia, fortunately, has a penknife, and although she at first resolves to kill herself rather than suffer dishonor, at the final moment she strikes at him in desperation and plunges the knife into his heart. Sophia, full of foreboding over the danger in which she has left her friend, arrives on the scene after the deed is done, takes care of the distraught Constantia, and transports her to England.

Artistic Failure

Such a denouement does irreparable harm to the book, for it resolves a serious intellectual and moral conflict by extraneous physical means. The conclusion, nonetheless, has had its defenders. Sydney J. Krause justifies it in terms of the novel's relation to contemporary tales of seduction, which, in his view, Brown far surpasses in his treatment of the subject. He created unusually endowed characters, put them at the end in a complex relation, and expressed through their confrontation radical ideas on sex and marriage that remain unrefuted.[17] Norman S. Grabo, on the other hand, approaching the book with assumptions drawn from twentieth-century psychology, minimizes the effect of the conclusion by presenting Ormond as "Constantia's erotic principle" that she must face and put down before she can unite "generative energy with chaste restraint" by "joining Sophia's existence to her own."[18] These interpretations have their interest, but each is bought at the price of ignoring the theme that Brown sets up in the book and develops through the interrelation of Constantia with the other major characters. This theme comes to naught at the end, and Constantia and Ormond, two highly original and interesting persons, are transformed into stock characters of melodramatic fiction.

Most of the damage is done to the characterization of Constantia, who up to this point has been presented as an intellectually strong and independent young woman. In her struggle against the physical troubles that beset the Dudley family, Constantia engages the reader's interest by her forthright yet feminine actions, and even in her first encounters with Ormond, she reveals a staunchness of character that is truly winning. But with the appearance of Sophia, who dominates her completely, Constantia seems to lose all individuality and become a mere puppet manipulated by her companion. Her final meeting with Ormond is even more unfortunate, for, as Warfel has observed, Constantia is not allowed to win the victory that by rights should be hers. Had Brown permitted her triumph to come through "a newly won religious faith," Constantia would certainly be a much greater heroine. To be sure, she "extricates herself in the successful resolution of the plot," but she should have been given the strength "to win her own victory, intellectually as well as physically."[19] As it is, her physical triumph robs her of what should have been an intellectual and moral one.

Indeed, for all her strengths and virtues, Constantia Dudley is in many ways a much less memorable character than Clara Wieland, who lays a more powerful hold on the imagination of the reader. Though Clara is at times overdrawn, her descent into madness is made thoroughly credible, and her intellectual and emotional problems are adequately dramatized. Seen in relation to Clara, Constantia is considerably paler. Her development is weaker, and her intellectual and moral struggle is hardly objectified at all. Besides, Constantia's relationship with Sophia leaves much to be desired, and some critics have commented upon its unhealthy aspects.[20] Though Sophia has recently married in Europe, she leaves her husband to search in America for her lost friend. Once she finds her, the two women become as close and secretive as lovers, and Courtland is only briefly mentioned again, even after the two women finally arrive in England. This point should not, however, be insisted upon, for Brown may only have intended to show the closeness of the tie that, considering the fact that the women were reared together, understandably binds them to one another. Yet at best, the relation is not one to increase the stature of Constantia as the heroine of the novel.

Much the same kind of criticism can be leveled against the characterization of Ormond. A believable villain in the early part of the tale, Ormond is well presented as a man who conceals his deceitful intent behind a pleasant external appearance. To the other characters in the novel, he appears to be an educated and urbane gentleman whose motives are always openly avowed, but as the action progresses, more of his true character is revealed. We gain an insight into his selfishness and want of compassion, for example, in his treatment of Helena Cleves and in his lack of remorse at her suicide, and we perceive his intellectual duplicity in his discussions with Constantia. We are hardly prepared, however, for his violent actions, insane bombast, and melodramatic posturing at the end of the book, where Brown converts him into a veritable madman. One could argue that a man of Ormond's principles might well descend to this kind of violence[21]—especially when we consider the tales that Sophia relates of his youth (2:263–64)—but the shift is not made with enough artistry to be wholly convincing. A character with Wieland's background and temperament may, under sufficient provocation, plausibly become a homicidal maniac without subtle transition; an astute and artful one like Ormond should not be changed so drastically without more adequate preparation.

The deterioration of the characters has a far-reaching effect on the meaning of the book, for the final struggle in which they engage seriously detracts from the theme that Brown seems to have been developing throughout the tale. The whole movement of the novel has been concerned with the value of Constantia's education in enabling her to survive the physical disasters that she encounters and her inability to win by herself the intellectual and moral battle against the unbelieving Ormond. Indeed, the introduction of the religious theme in the latter half of the book seems to indicate that *Ormond,* like *Wieland,* suggests the need for religious training in the education of the young. Certainly the absence of religion in Constantia's background reminds one of a similar lack in the education of the Wielands. If, as Brown clearly suggests, his theme concerns the importance of a religious view of the world as the guide to life, one could wish that he had dramatized the conflict more fully and made the religious element more important in the final resolution.

In this respect, the novel is curiously like *Wieland*: both leave the affirmation of value disturbingly vague. To be sure, *Ormond* is considerably more specific, but it fails to say precisely what the religious view should be. Sophia clearly affirms her belief in a divinely directed and purposeful universe, and she looks forward to an afterlife "where woes are at an end and virtue finds its recompence" (2:239). Her God, however, is most often referred to, in deistic terms, as "the great author of being and felicity" (2:224) or as "a divine and omniscient observer" (2:262), and religion itself is hardly felt as a powerful or dramatic force in the novel. It is asserted as a value rather than lived as a belief. Hence, the reader leaves the novel with a feeling that Brown has not fully expressed his theme, that something more than a general affirmation is needed to make the novel really effective. The book remains interesting for the light it sheds on the development of Brown's thought during his career as a novelist, but it leaves much to be desired as a work of art.

Yet despite the poorly resolved theme and the bungled conclusion, *Ormond,* like *Wieland,* shows signs of Brown's unmistakable talent. Both books are uneven, and their strengths and weaknesses differ. Although in overall structure, *Ormond* may be considered superior to *Wieland* in that it contains no poorly handled subplot left incomplete until the end, it exhibits a number of inconsistencies in detail, most probably the result, as Paul C. Rodgers, Jr., has observed, of Brown's improvisations as he tried to keep his writing abreast of the press. Indeed, he even lifted a passage bodily out of his already published "The Man at Home" when he apparently ran short of material. By doing so, he created problems for his book when Ursula Monrose of that section later turns up as the very different Martinette de Beauvais.[22] Whatever its flaws, however, *Ormond* remains a very readable and, on the whole, a coherent novel. The faults lie mainly, as Warfel has suggested, in the imbalance of episodes which are in themselves structurally important and pertinent to the meaning.[23] Except for these errors in relative development and emphasis, the action of *Ormond* is, in general, rather well conceived and, up to a point, well executed.

Ormond is also superior to *Wieland* in the use Brown makes of realistic detail to establish the social environment in which his characters move. Apart from the Gothic enclosures, the physical setting is not of much importance in *Wieland,* nor do the characters exist in any recognizable social context. In *Ormond* they live and act in a society that becomes most real and immediate when the yellow fever strikes Philadelphia. Through the use of detail—the rumble of wagon wheels through the city at night, "the shrieks and laments of survivors," the gaunt and gummy-eyed horse standing quietly before a house while a coffin is brought out—Brown evokes a sense of the stricken town (2:53, 58, 41). He manages to render credible, too, the sufferings of the dying and the terror of those who desert their relatives in the city only to perish, feared and shunned, in the countryside (2:47–52). These scenes are not presented in as much circumstantial detail as one might expect to find in later realists, and they represent only a small portion of the book, but they clearly reveal a talent for the realistic in Brown that one might not expect from a reading of *Wieland.*

In point of view and style, on the other hand, *Ormond* is by far the weaker novel. Less central to the action in *Ormond* than Clara Wieland was in the previous novel, Sophia Courtland hardly functions as a character at all throughout most of the book. Indeed, she serves little more aesthetic purpose than would an omniscient narrator, and Brown makes no attempt to exploit the point of view for dramatic—or Gothic—effect as he had in *Wieland.* The point of view has an important effect on style, for the language of *Ormond* is quieter in tone than that of the earlier book. The reason is not far to seek: the kind of prose that is appropriate to the emotionally distraught Clara would be totally unsuited to the rather staid, proper Sophia. The point of view in *Ormond,* moreover, has its effect on our perception of Constantia. We do not experience the vicissitudes of her fortune as we do Clara Wieland's, nor are we ever caught up so much in her story. All that we know of her comes through Sophia. Because of the change in point of view and style, *Ormond* inevitably lacks the immediacy and suspense of *Wieland.*

Taking the two on balance, one must conclude that *Ormond* is not so successful as *Wieland.* Its virtues are relatively minor. Realistic detail of the plague-ridden city does not make up for the utter collapse of characterization and thematic development at the end of the book, and a straight—and essentially simple—line of action is really no suitable substitute for the gripping story developed in the major part of the earlier novel. Carwin is, in many ways, a much more interesting villain than Ormond, and Theodore Wieland is a far more credible madman. In its broader aspects, too, the earlier book is more satisfying. Although both are intellectually incomplete, *Wieland* explores its problem more dramatically, and despite the Gothic melodrama of the mysterious voices, it actually does so in a much more convincing action. The opposition of forces is much too neat in *Ormond* so that the story appears contrived. In the light of such evidence, one can only conclude that, although *Ormond* certainly contributes much to our understanding of Brown's themes and his mode of expression, the book falls far short of the not inconsiderable artistic success that he had achieved in *Wieland.*

Chapter Four
Arthur Mervyn

In December 1798, before he had finished *Ormond,* Brown wrote his brother Armitt that he had agreed with a Philadelphia publisher to complete *Arthur Mervyn,*[1] a book that already had a considerable history. It may have been begun as early as 1795, when Brown is known to have been at work on a "Philadelphia novel," and the first nine chapters had appeared in the Philadelphia *Weekly Magazine* between 16 June and 25 August 1798, when the onset of the yellow fever forced the journal to suspend publication. How much additional manuscript may still have been in hand at this point is not known, but Norman S. Grabo has made a persuasive case for the hypothesis that Brown may already have written the next three chapters. These complete the confession of Welbeck, and since the continuity of his story is unbroken through chapter 12, it seems reasonable to assume that Brown had written the whole segment before publication ceased. With chapter 13, however, the book takes off in a different direction. "The nature of this break" and "the new material introduced" at this point suggest, in Grabo's words, "a later period of writing than the first twelve chapters."[2]

How much later cannot now be determined, for surviving evidence is inconclusive. The most we can say is that chapter 16, which describes the career and death of Maravegli, could not have been written before 17 September, for the character is modeled on Joseph B. Scandella, a patient of Smith who died in New York on that date. Since Brown spent nearly a month with William Dunlap in Perth Amboy recuperating from his illness, it is possible, as Grabo suggests, that Brown worked on *Arthur Mervyn* during his convalescence, composing those chapters that describe the horrors of plague-ridden Philadelphia, events that were certainly "fresh in his mind" at the time.[3] But there is no hard evidence to support the conjecture, and the chapters could have been written much later, in January, for example, after Brown had completed *Ormond.* By 20 December Brown had already agreed with Hugh Maxwell to bring *Arthur Mervyn* to completion, and he delayed the work only because *Ormond* was occupying his time. Once that book was finished, Brown turned his attention to *Arthur Mervyn* and completed the first volume in five or six weeks. By 10 February he was done. Maxwell published the book "sometime between 7 March and 21 May 1799."[4]

Even less is known about the composition and publication of the second part of the novel. Before he had finished writing the first, Brown was aware that "a second part or sequel" would be necessary, and he left a sufficient opening for the continuation of the story.[5] But Brown did not write it immediately. During the spring and summer of 1799, he was occupied with other affairs, particularly the composition of *Edgar Huntly,* the first volume of which appeared during the summer. It is not until the following spring that we again hear of *Arthur Mervyn,* when Brown writes of it as if the composition were already well advanced. Dissatisfied with Maxwell's handling of his books, Brown accepted his brother James's advice to seek a New York publisher for the second part. Hocquet Caritat was then in England, and Brown made arrangements with George F. Hopkins, a New York printer, for the publication of the book. When it appeared is not certain—perhaps "as early as 4 July {or} as late as 3 September" 1800—but Grabo is probably right in accepting a date toward the latter end of that period. In the August issue of his *Monthly Magazine,* Brown himself lists the book as just published.[6]

Because *Arthur Mervyn* was written in at least three segments over a period of nearly two years, it suffers more than do Brown's other novels from his practice of improvising as he wrote. The story is straightforward enough. It presents a young man's rise from rural poverty and ignorance to a degree of urban affluence and experience in society. We must, in other words, consider the two volumes as a reasonably unified whole. But the second part moves to a conclusion that is demonstrably different from what Brown originally intended, and he handles the point of view in such a way as to create ambiguities about the young man's character. The problem of appearance that the novel presents is so intense that no consensus has yet been reached on its meaning. Critics have aligned themselves in opposing positions, each of which can be defended from both internal and external evidence.[7] In view of this critical controversy, it is best, perhaps, to take up each part of the book separately. In that way we can see what Brown accomplished in the first part of *Arthur Mervyn* before we examine the change of direction that occurs in the second.

The First Part

Part 1 of *Arthur Mervyn* has long been praised for its graphic descriptions of the plague, material that Brown knew from his own experience, perhaps in Philadelphia in 1793[8] and certainly in New York in 1798. Although he had used this material for some of the most effective scenes in *Ormond,* those in *Arthur Mervyn* are by far the better. Death and desolation hang over the city like a pall, and as Mervyn moves through the almost deserted streets, we get a keen sense of the horror of the place. Some of the episodes are extremely well done—as is the scene, justly praised by Clark as an example of "Brown's power," in which the hearse drivers with businesslike efficiency go about their job of collecting bodies from the houses.[9] So inured have they become to human suffering that they are only momentarily concerned that the last victim was not yet dead when they thrust him into his coffin (3:140). The circumstantial manner in which the episode is told and the rather detached attitude that Brown maintains in describing it remind one of the technique of Ernest Hemingway. Such objectively presented scenes are by no means common in Brown, who tends rather to overplay, but they are, for that reason, the more effective when they do appear.

More typical of Brown's style is the Gothic horror he includes. In one episode, Mervyn awakes from a blow on the head to find some strangers about to place him in a coffin, and he shudders to think how close he came to premature burial (3:148–49). Even more terrible is Brown's depiction of the hospital at Bushhill, a chamber of horrors where people dread to be taken. It is run by degenerate wretches who are tempted to work by the enormous wages paid them but who ignore the sick and carouse in their private apartments. Their laughter can be heard in the upper rooms, where a dying man cries out for water or begs for help to change his position so that he need not face "the ghastly writhings or deathful *smile* of his neighbour." Occasionally someone enters, and a body is dragged across the floor to a waiting coffin—a fate that lies in store for most of the sick who are brought there. Many of those who are stricken, therefore, hide themselves "in garrets and cellars and stables" to die in peace rather than face such horrors (3:173–74).

Brown's picture of plague-ridden Philadelphia is thus detailed and effective, but it is a mistake to assume, with some of the critics, that the realism of the plague scenes is their main value.[10] Realistic though they may be, their primary function in the novel is a symbolic one; they help to define one aspect of a city environment that, as two critics have argued, serves a thematic purpose in the novel. To Lewis, the city of Philadelphia is an "impenetrable network of secret and corrupt liaisons" into which the innocent young country boy makes his way, only to discover "the prolific reality of evil in every imaginable moral and physical form." To Berthoff, the "cruel and poisonous city world" that Mervyn enters is set against "an unpolluted countryside of farms and freemen" and serves as a point of contrast to "the

Jeffersonian hinterland" from which the hero originally comes and into which, after his first experience, he escapes. Too much, of course, can be made of this contrast, for Brown, as Berthoff correctly observes, is no doctrinaire agrarian in this book.[11] Nonetheless, the commercial city, both before and during the plague, does assume symbolic import as the place of Mervyn's adventures. The scenes of the plague, therefore, reinforce the concept of the corrupt city, an important element in the early part of the book.

Seen in these terms, *Arthur Mervyn* is a story of initiation,[12] not unlike *Ormond* in that it confronts an innocent character with physical and moral evil and shows the manner in which he comes to grips with it. Yet Arthur Mervyn is not merely another Constantia Dudley. Rather, he is an ambitious young man eager to make his way in the world, and as he works his way through the urban environment, its value begins to appear more positive. At first, however, Mervyn is almost destroyed by the evil he encounters. When we first meet him in the opening chapter of the book, he is deathly ill with the yellow fever. He is found by Doctor Stevens outside a house, his head sunk against the wall, his body held upright only by the cellar door against which he leans. Mervyn, we later learn, has contracted the disease on his second trip to the city. Nursed back to health by the doctor, who takes him in, Mervyn eventually recovers. He is recognized, however, by a Mr. Wortley as having been an associate of Thomas Welbeck, whose failure in business almost brought Wortley to ruin and who was last seen in Mervyn's company. Wortley suspects that Welbeck has absconded, and Mervyn is brought under suspicion of wrongdoing when he refuses to reveal anything of Welbeck's concerns.

Fortunately for Mervyn, Doctor Stevens does not act on Wortley's suspicions without giving the young man a chance to defend his actions, and much of the story that follows is Mervyn's account of his past. He tells the doctor and his wife that he decided to leave his rural home when his father married a sluttish milkmaid who turned her husband against his son, and thrown on his own devices, the frail young man, who did not expect to live beyond a few more years,[13] set out alone to make his way in the city. From the very beginning, his experiences are uniformly unfortunate. His first night in town leaves him stripped of both money and possessions, and he soon finds himself, thoroughly gulled, alone in a closet in a strange house where a young man has taken him with the promise of a bed but where he is deserted for a practical joke. Mervyn's position is no laughing matter; were he to be found in the closet by the man and woman who go to sleep in the next room, he would be in serious trouble. Through his own courage and resourcefulness, however, he manages to escape, though he leaves his shoes behind when he does so. Barefoot and destitute, he intends to return to the country at once, but he is distracted from his purpose when he meets Welbeck, who, seeing a use for the boy, takes him into his house as a kind of copyist or scrivener and starts Mervyn along the path to success.

The story that follows is so complicated that it almost defies summary, yet the complex action must be recounted if the meaning of the book is to be fully understood. Suffice it to say that Welbeck is a villain whose past includes betrayal of a friend's trust, seduction of a married woman, and the consequent destruction of a whole family. Now engaged in some commercial dealings in Philadelphia, Welbeck is obsessed with the idea of maintaining a proper appearance in the world and is more concerned with what people think of him than with what he has done. Like all of Brown's other villains, he has a great thirst for knowledge and is familiar with "enlightened" principles (3:85). Like them, he does not scruple to use others for his own ends. He seduces Clemenza Lodi, who has fallen into his power, and he frankly informs Mervyn at one point that, by taking him into his service, he intended to do him an injury as well as to confer a benefit (3:85). Welbeck differs from Carwin, Ludloe, and Ormond in that he is engaged in no wildly utopian schemes; he is, when we first meet him, absorbed in what appears to be a normal commercial enterprise. His desire to figure largely in the world and to maintain the kind of appearance that commands respect is at least more recognizably human than the other villains' vaunting ambitions.

For a time Welbeck is able to deceive his business associates by the lordly appearance he maintains, but his resources are not nearly so great as he would have people believe. Utterly averse to labor, he tries to keep up his appearance and to replenish his stock of funds by plunging heavily, partly on borrowed money, in a maritime enterprise that seems impossible of failure. The unforeseen event occurs that frustrates all his plans, and Welbeck is brought to ruin. At the same time, Amos Watson, the sea-captain brother of the married woman whom Welbeck had corrupted, appears on the scene and challenges him to a strange duel to which Welbeck agrees only when it seems that Watson will let him live solely for the purpose of destroying his reputation. By an odd chance, the carefully aimed bullet of Watson misses its mark, but Welbeck's random shot kills the captain. At this point, Mervyn, who has served Welbeck unquestioningly for several days, comes upon his master, and, promising never to reveal what Welbeck tells him, he learns the history of his past. Mervyn helps his master bury Watson in the cellar of the house and agrees to row him across the Delaware River. Two hundred yards from shore, however, Welbeck leaps overboard; Mervyn, unable to save him, believes that he has committed suicide.

Only five days have elapsed since Mervyn came to the city, but, as he tells his auditors, he had "gathered more instruction [from them] than from the whole tissue of [his] previous existence" (3:120). He has been initiated into the corrupt ways of the commercial city, for he learns in serving Welbeck much of the machinations of the business community and has even caught wind of a plot among some of Welbeck's associates to defraud him of a large sum of money. He has seen in Welbeck the contrast between the wealthy, important man he seems to be and the unscrupulous villain that he actually is, and he has also witnessed his act of despair when faced with financial ruin and public exposure. Thus, Mervyn's education in the ways of the world has begun, and to a great extent he is shaken by his experience, because his main desire after Welbeck's apparent suicide is to flee the city. Before the first light of day, he is on his way once more to the country, taking with him from Welbeck's house only a book, written in Italian, that had belonged to Clemenza Lodi's brother.

Part of Mervyn's urge to leave the city results from his fear of what might happen to him if he should remain, part from a desire to find a place where he can exchange his labor for the necessities of life. He turns to the country, then, as his "sole asylum" (3:118), and he soon falls in with the Hadwins, a Quaker family whose simple life in the rural countryside stands in strong contrast to everything that he has experienced in the city. "The manners of this family," he observes, "quiet, artless, and cordial, the occupations allotted me, the land by which the dwelling was surrounded, its pure airs, romantic walks, and exhaustless fertility, constituted a powerful contrast to the scenes which I had left behind, and were congenial with every dictate of my understanding and every sentiment that glowed in my heart." Hadwin himself combines "the simplicity of the husbandman and the devotion of the Quaker . . . with humanity and intelligence"; and his daughters, Susan and Eliza, though "strangers to the benefits of an elaborate education," had made good use of the instruction they had received and were totally "unacquainted with calamity and vice, through the medium of either observation or books" (3:123–24). Indeed, so sharp is the contrast between the virtues of the Hadwins and the venality of Mervyn's associates in Philadelphia that he seems on the point of affirming a belief in the complete superiority of country life.

His rural idyll is soon disturbed by a series of events that leads him back to the city—and, in time, to a considerably different opinion. In perusing Lodi's book, he discovers some twenty thousand dollars in banknotes glued between the pages. Though tempted at first to keep the money, Mervyn correctly reasons that it is not really his but belongs to Clemenza Lodi. He determines to seek out the girl, who, having become pregnant by Welbeck, had been sent from town, Mervyn knows not where. But before he can embark on his search, yellow fever strikes Philadelphia. The Hadwin family is seriously distressed at the news, because Susan's fiancé, a man named Wallace, works in the city.[14] When, after a series of letters, Wallace fails to come and nothing further is heard from him, Mervyn decides to go in search of him. Though aware of the danger he incurs, he willingly accepts it in the belief that, because of his constitutional weakness, he will not live long anyway and may at least die helping others. By indirect questioning, he learns from Hadwin the name of the man for whom Wallace works (it turns out to be an associate of Welbeck), and unbeknown to the Hadwins, Mervyn sets off for the city on a dual mission: to locate Wallace and, if possible, to learn the whereabouts of Clemenza Lodi so that he can give her the money that is rightfully hers.

Mervyn's second experience in Philadelphia continues his initiation into the realities of city life. Some are harsh. He learns that Wallace was almost destroyed by the self-seeking of his employer, who delayed his departure from Philadelphia because he feared for his business, and he sees for himself both the callousness of the hearse drivers and the hardheartedness of innkeepers who will admit no one into their hostels. Yet others are more positive. Some men are capable of great benevolence: Maravegli, who lost his life while trying to help others; Estwick, who saves Mervyn from being encoffined alive; Medlicote, who at one point takes him into his house and offers him food and shelter; and Doctor Stevens, who saves his life when he falls sick with the fever. Thus, Mervyn gains a new insight into the city. As he later tells the doctor, in his first encounter with city life he "had met with nothing but scenes of folly, depravity and cunning," but in his second trip to Philadelphia he met a number of honest and admirable men and began to understand the intellectual values fostered by urban life (3:293). Though the physical evil he encounters is almost overwhelming, his experience shows him too the more praiseworthy side of the city.

At the moment, Mervyn is concerned only with his immediate problems as he tries to fulfill the purposes that brought him into Philadelphia, and despite the hardships he faces, he achieves part of his goal. He manages to locate the unfortunate Wallace, who was sent to the hospital against his will by his panic-stricken employer and who unexpectedly survived his stay of several days in that horrible place. Indeed, Mervyn persuades the weakened Wallace to try to leave the city, and after walking as far as they can, he even procures him transportation to the country in a passing chaise. By this time, Mervyn has himself contracted the disease. Unable to make his way to any place where he might find asylum and fearing that he will be taken to the hospital if he remains in the streets, he decides to hide in Welbeck's house, where he unexpectedly finds himself at the moment of near exhaustion. Here he prepares to wait out the disease or to die unmolested. Much to his surprise, Mervyn once again encounters Welbeck, who, it turns out, was unable to kill himself by drowning and who, suddenly realizing that some unaccounted-for money must be concealed in Lodi's book, has returned to the city to seek it.

Mervyn and Welbeck inevitably come into sharp conflict over the money, for, with his knowledge of Welbeck's character, Mervyn no longer cooperates with but directly opposes him. He foresees that Welbeck would only use the money for "the purpose of selfishness and misery" (3:199), whereas he will return it to Clemenza Lodi, who needs it. The naive Mervyn, however, is no match for the unscrupulous Welbeck. Though Welbeck's passionate rage is unable to break down his resolve, Mervyn falls prey to the other's shrewdness. Welbeck convinces him that the notes are forged and that Mervyn will only cause trouble if he gives them to Clemenza. The gullible young man believes the story because it is told "with every token of sincerity" (3:208–9). When Welbeck turns away for a moment, Mervyn quickly burns them lest they cause trouble to others. Utterly appalled by this act, Welbeck reveals that they were real after all, and in his rage, he would probably have done Mervyn violence had not people been heard outside who, both of them think, are coming in search of the sick. Welbeck escapes, and Mervyn, though desperately ill, avoids the searchers and attempts to make his way to Medlicote's house. Missing the direction, he sinks to the ground at the spot where Doctor Stevens eventually finds him and takes him in.

The first part of the novel ends at precisely the spot where it began, and, except for the loose threads that Brown consciously left untied, can be read as a completed work. The volume does indeed have a kind of thematic unity, for it details the initiation of a naif into the ways of a world that almost overwhelms him with its duplicity and physical danger. His experience is valuable, for it illustrates to him something of the relative values of city and country life and prepares him to take his place in the world. If we read the book in these terms, Mervyn is seen as a rather conventional hero, a virtuous young man who derives instruction from his experience and resolves, as he does in the final paragraph in the volume, to show his gratitude to those who have befriended him by dedicating his life to worthwhile purposes. Such a conclusion leaves little place for the story to go, except to illustrate the various acts by which the virtuous Mervyn keeps his resolve, and, indeed, something of this sort seems to have been Brown's original purpose.

In a letter he wrote to his brother James in February 1799, Brown makes clear that he at first intended the second part of the novel to illustrate the virtue of his hero in overcoming the impediments and trials placed in his path. James Brown had objected to the incident, toward the end of part 1, in which Mervyn burns the twenty thousand dollars he had found in Lodi's book, but the author defends the episode by arguing that the money must be destroyed because Mervyn "is intended as a hero whose virtue, in order to be productive of benefit to others, and felicity to himself, stands in no need of riches." Indeed, in the plot line Brown describes, Mervyn not only triumphs over adversity but returns to Eliza Hadwin, who, having inherited the farm from her now-dead father and sister, marries the hero and thus presents him with "the rewards of virtue."[15] But although the second part of *Arthur Mervyn* does indeed begin as if it were to follow the plan that Brown sketched in his letter, it eventually comes to such a radically different conclusion that we must defer a final interpretation of either part until both have been duly considered.

The Second Part

The second part of *Arthur Mervyn* begins with a series of adventures that the hero, now recovered from the yellow fever, engages in as he tries to act the part of benefactor to others. At first his acts are perfectly reasonable. Deeply concerned about the fate of both Wallace and the Hadwins, Mervyn leaves the city after he is cured to visit them, only to learn that disaster has struck their rural idyll. Although Wallace had been brought to a country house where he had recovered his strength, he never returned to the Hadwin farm but disappeared. Hadwin, who had gone into the city during the plague to seek Wallace, had himself contracted the disease and died. Susan expires soon after Mervyn arrives at the farm, and the younger daughter, Eliza, to whom Mervyn is attracted, loses her inheritance to a violent and brutal uncle—exemplifying the less attractive side of rural life[16]—who holds a mortgage upon it. Mervyn is thus given ample opportunity to help Eliza by practicing the benevolence he feels he is obligated to show to all, but he soon becomes such an officious busybody as he goes about doing good to others that the reader begins to view him in an increasingly unfavorable light.

Mervyn embarks on an astonishing career of meddling in other people's lives. He finds a country home for Eliza to stay in, and, although he no longer has her money, he goes off in search of Clemenza Lodi, who, he has learned from Doctor Stevens, had been placed by Welbeck in a house of ill repute. He invades the house to find the girl; meets Mrs. Achsa Fielding, who, unaware of the profession of her companions, has spent the night visiting there; urges her to leave; attempts to help Clemenza; and almost gets shot for his pains. He learns from Clemenza that Welbeck is in debtors' prison, and, much to his erstwhile master's rage, he seeks him out and moralizes upon him, even bringing in Doctor Stevens to try to help the man. From Welbeck, who is on the point of death, they learn of a money belt that Watson wore on his body and that Welbeck has taken from the exhumed corpse. With this belt, which Welbeck surrenders, Mervyn is off to Baltimore to restore what is due the Watson family and some people named Maurice, who have a claim on the money. He performs the task with evident self-satisfaction, but he is somewhat abashed that the Maurices are not so grateful to him as he thinks they should be.

Back in Philadelphia, Mervyn continues his impetuous—almost compulsive—course of action. He succeeds in finding a refuge for Clemenza Lodi and manages to persuade Mrs. Fielding to provide a home for Eliza Hadwin. The more he sees of Mrs. Fielding, the more he becomes enamored of her, and as the novel approaches its end, it soon becomes apparent that he is going to marry Achsa Fielding, a widow and a mother some six years his senior, who turns out to be a Jewess and whom Mervyn calls his "good mamma" (3:407). The novel ends with the hero rapturously looking forward to his impending marriage.

The conclusion of the tale reveals an Arthur Mervyn considerably different from the lad who walked into Philadelphia one night, only to become the butt of a practical joke, and who became the easy dupe of Thomas Welbeck. Indeed, he is not the same young man whom Doctor Stevens found in the street and nursed back to health, and he is certainly not the hero Brown intended to develop in his original plans for the second part of the book. Mervyn has rejected Eliza Hadwin as a wife, and although he does embark on a career of doing good to others, he proceeds in so compulsive and self-righteous a fashion that the reader is hard-pressed to admire his virtue. To be sure, the later Mervyn is implicit in the first, and he remains to the end something of a naive boy. But there is in addition, as many critics have now recognized, an unattractive aspect to Mervyn's character that is fully revealed only as the second volume progresses.[17]

This is not to say that Mervyn's character is inconsistent or that it changes sharply during the course of the narrative. If we look back into the first part of the novel, we find elements in his personality that make his later development both credible and consistent. There is, for example, Mervyn's attitude toward the women he meets. As one would expect of an eighteen year old, he becomes enamored of each in turn, but with each he entertains hopes of material success. When he first falls in with Welbeck, Mervyn begins to dream that the older man might adopt him as a son, an idea he seriously considers because "wealth has ever been capriciously distributed" and sometimes results from a "trivial and fallacious" cause (3:57–58). In addition, he observes that his appearance, resembling as it does that of her brother, has visibly affected Clemenza Lodi. Since they both live in Welbeck's house, they will inevitably be thrown together. "Time," he thinks, "would lay level impediments and establish familiarity, and this intercourse might foster love and terminate in—*marriage!*" (3:58). In this connection, Mervyn has not yet looked upon marriage as a step toward material well-being, but both ideas occur to him almost simultaneously at a time when he scarcely knows either Welbeck or Clemenza—indeed when he has just met them. The dreams, in fact, sound suspiciously like those of an ambitious young man intent on achieving wealth and position in the world.

Such a conclusion is supported by subsequent developments. Once he learns of Welbeck's disaster and of his relations with Clemenza, Mervyn, understandably enough, thinks no more of achieving success through them. Instead, he leaves the city and associates himself with the Hadwins. Again he meets a young woman, Eliza Hadwin, with whom he quickly becomes enamored. Eliza clearly returns his affection, but when Mervyn begins to think of the future, certain doubts immediately cross his mind. His own labors are light and earn him sufficient subsistence for himself, but they would not suffice if he were married. Besides, though Hadwin's farm supports the family adequately, "divided between his children [it] would be too scanty for either." It is only when his thoughts reach this point that he remembers another obstacle—that the Hadwins are Quakers, a sect that forbade marriage with one of another belief. Mervyn seriously tells us that he is incapable of hypocrisy, that he would not have attempted to change his opinions or to feign a conversion himself even "if the possession of all that ambition can conceive, were added to the transports of union with Eliza Hadwin" (3:124–25). Mervyn may be perfectly sincere in his statement, but the reader observes that he makes it only after he has decided that marriage with Eliza would offer him no hope for material improvement.

Indeed, as conditions change, so also do Mervyn's opinions, and we are not surprised when, in the second part of the novel, he returns to the Hadwin farm and begins to see things in quite a different light. With

Susan and her father both dead, Eliza will apparently inherit the farm, and since Eliza is now alone in the world, Mervyn does not think that anyone will be hurt if she marries out of her faith. He is also quick to observe that his "own interest could not fail to recommend a scheme by which the precious benefits of competence and independence might be honestly obtained" (3:291). That Mervyn does not rush into marriage is no proof that he is not self-seeking. He clearly foresees that opportunity might be greater for him in the city, and he wants to defer his decision until he has tasted the fruits of the better side of city life. He soon finds out, moreover, that the farm, which figured so largely in his thoughts, will revert to Eliza's uncle and the girl will be left almost destitute. This information, Mervyn reveals, "necessarily produced a change in my views with regard to my friend" (3:311) for, although he had previously promised to bring her to the city, he now places her in a house in the country. Such an act is dictated by economic necessity since her means of subsistence are now so small, and he does eventually persuade Mrs. Fielding to take her in. But Mervyn loses interest in Eliza in the ensuing episodes, and one suspects that her poverty is at least partly the reason.

The final outcome of the novel surely confirms the reader's suspicions, for Mervyn soon shifts his affections to Mrs. Achsa Fielding, the woman he ultimately marries.[18] Once again he believes that there are good reasons for his decision. Eliza Hadwin is still very young, and Mervyn argues that she does not have "that solidity of mind; that maturity of intelligence" he needs in a wife (3:405). Older, better educated, and more sophisticated, Mrs. Fielding does. But she is also financially well off. Shortly after he meets her, Mervyn learns that she possesses a "considerable, and even splendid fortune" (3:415). That Mervyn takes this fact into consideration is clear enough in the novel. When he discusses his emotional life with Doctor Stevens, the older man points out as a disadvantage to their union that Achsa Fielding "is a foreigner: independent of controul, and rich." Mervyn's reply is revealing: "All which, are blessings to herself and to him for whom her hand is reserved; especially if like me, he is indigent" (3:432). It is too much to say, perhaps, that Mervyn deliberately marries money, but the fact that material gain is never far from his mind when he contemplates marriage is surely significant.[19]

It is not only his attitude toward women that reveals the less attractive side of Mervyn's character; his ability to attach himself to an older person who can provide him with the means for material success is nothing short of uncanny. Mervyn comes under the influence of three older men in the story, and with each he manages to advance his career by simply being whatever the other person wants him to be. "A chameleon of convenient virtue," as Berthoff describes him, Mervyn assumes "the form and role that others wish him to assume."[20] This remarkable talent is apparent from the very beginning and is symbolized first by Mervyn's simply donning a suit of clothes. When Welbeck meets Mervyn on the boy's first morning in the city and, seeing a use for him, asks him to come to his house, Mervyn eagerly assents and is duly impressed by the opulence of the residence. Offered a job as a scribe, he immediately accepts, moves into Welbeck's house, and puts on the clothes offered him. His reactions once he dons his clothes—items he describes in loving detail—reveal a great deal about his character.

"Appearances," Mervyn states, "are wonderfully influenced by dress"—a true enough observation, but he seems to confuse the appearance he now presents with reality. Much taken by the figure he pictures himself as cutting—"so well proportioned, so galant, and so graceful"—he can scarcely believe he is the same person. "Twenty minutes ago," he says as he looks out the window, "I was traversing that path a barefoot beggar; now I am thus. Again I surveyed myself. Surely some insanity has fastened on my understanding. My senses are the sport of dreams. Some magic that disdains the cumbrousness of nature's progress, has wrought this change" (3:51). So much does Mervyn become what his clothes symbolize that he willingly makes himself the instrument of Welbeck's desires. At his master's request, he agrees to speak of his past with no one but Welbeck, and he even asks for specific instructions on what his master wishes him to conceal. Mervyn is soon rendered uneasy by the promise he has made, but as he tells his listeners, "these inquietudes . . . were transient" (3:63). He becomes what Welbeck wishes him to be and seems ready to assume that his new, fancy clothes have wrought a real change in him.

So superficial is the change, however, that it can be put off once again with the clothes. Once he believes that Welbeck is drowned in the Delaware River, he sees the necessity of becoming once more what he was when he first entered the city. The transformation is easily effected. He returns to his chamber in Welbeck's house, disrobes, and resumes his "check shirt, and trowsers, and fustian coat. This change being accomplished, nothing remained," he states, "but that I should strike into the country with the utmost expedition" (3:119). A simple country man again after his sojourn in the city, Mervyn immediately attaches himself to the first man he meets, Mr. Hadwin, whose benevolence so fills him with "gratitude and joy" that he is willing to become a son to him: "Methought I could embrace him as a father, and entrance into his house, appeared like return to a long-lost and much-loved home. My desolate and lonely condition appeared to be changed for paternal regards and the tenderness of friendship" (3:123). Mervyn is probably sincere as he says these words, for nowhere is there evidence that he is a deliberate sharper. But at the same time, the reader inevitably wonders at his ability to land on his feet.

Nor is this the last convenient change that Mervyn manages to make; the second part of the novel continues the development that can be discerned in the first. After his second trip to the city, Mervyn again attaches himself to an older man who is willing to befriend him. Doctor Stevens not only nurses the young man back to health after his serious illness but, after he has heard his story, also entertains the idea of taking him into his family to teach him the science of medicine (3:220). No sooner is the subject broached to Mervyn than he enthusiastically accepts, his eyes sparkling with pleasure. Indeed, he even manages to make his acceptance sound as if he were conferring a favor on his benefactor, for, he avers, "if my pride should refuse [the offer], I should prove myself less worthy than you think, and give you pain, instead of that pleasure which I am bound to confer" (3:224). This speech is brilliant because it clearly reveals the degree to which the remarkable Arthur Mervyn succeeds in gaining a personal advantage while professing to his benefactor the most unselfish of motives and the sincerest of intentions.

The reader is hardly surprised, therefore, when Arthur makes his final move and connects himself with Mrs. Fielding, a woman, who, as Berthoff observes, can, like Welbeck—and for that matter, one might add, Hadwin and Stevens—give Mervyn what he wants at little cost to himself.[21] Just as he had done before with the older men, he adjusts himself to her wishes. "As to me, I was wax in her hand," he writes. "Without design and without effort, I was always of that form she wished me to assume" (3:428). By this time the reader is fully aware that herein lies Mervyn's great talent: his happiness is forever tied up in the wishes of others, and he is always willing to subordinate his apparent will to their desires. In each case, and above all in the last, he manages to profit by the connection. Indeed, with Mrs. Fielding, he acquires a wife and a "good mamma" at the same time. Moreover, she is rich and he is poor, yet at one point he pursues her with the constant reiteration of the question: "Tell me how I shall serve you? What can I do to make you happier? Poor am I in every thing but zeal, but still I may do something. What—pray tell me what can I do?" (3:429). Though part of Mervyn's importunity may derive from his apparent innocence, one implication is certainly clear: he will once again confer a benefit by accepting the gifts of another.

The True Character of Mervyn

In the light of such evidence, it seems obvious to conclude that there is a side to Mervyn's character that he does not consciously reveal but which is present, at least potentially, from the very beginning of the novel. It is one that even his friends fail to recognize, for Mervyn—like Welbeck before his financial disaster—makes a very attractive appearance and maintains a presence that wins completely many of those who have to deal with him. Doctor Stevens, for example, is strongly attracted to Mervyn from the first moment they meet because of his "simple and ingenuous" aspect, and he informs the reader that he "scarcely ever beheld an object which laid so powerful and sudden a claim to [his] affection and succour" (3:6). The influence that Mervyn acquires over the doctor is increased by the story he relates. When Mr. Wortley warns Stevens against him, the doctor quite correctly believes that Mervyn should be given a chance to defend himself, but he and his wife are already favorably disposed to hear what Mervyn has to say, and Mrs. Stevens in particular "was prepared to hear and to forgive the errors of inexperience and precipitation" (3:16) before she has even had a chance to learn what they might be.

When Mervyn finishes recounting his experiences—it takes him all of part 1 to do so—Doctor Stevens immediately accepts his story as the truth, purely on the basis of his own word. It occurs to the doctor, especially on Wortley's prompting, that Mervyn's story could be a tissue of lies. The doctor is a man of experience and knows full well that "a smooth exterior, a show of virtue, and a specious tale, are, a thousand times, exhibited in human intercourse by craft and subtlety." But although these thoughts do come to his mind and although he makes an attempt to corroborate Mervyn's account, Doctor Stevens never really doubts that Mervyn is telling the truth, even when other people call his character into question. What convinces the doctor is the manner in which Mervyn tells his story and the way he looks when he recounts it. "Had I heard Mervyn's story from another, or read it in a book," the doctor asserts, "I might, perhaps, have found it possible to suspect the truth; but, as long as the impression, made by his tones, gestures and looks, remained in my memory, this suspicion was impossible. . . . He that listens to his words may question their truth, but he that looks upon his countenance when speaking, cannot withhold his faith" (3:229–30).

Other people, however, are not so ready to credit Mervyn's tale solely on the basis of his candid face and glib tongue. Wortley continues to warn his friend against placing confidence in the "smooth features and fluent accents" of his protégé (3:249), and Mrs. Wentworth, a mature woman who had good reason to suspect that Mervyn was in league with Welbeck, informs him on one occasion that, although she cannot positively disbelieve his story, she will not bestow her faith on his tale without objective evidence. For, she tells him, "there must be other proofs besides an innocent brow and a voluble tongue, to make me give full credit to your pretensions." She is willing to lay aside her suspicions that he has been "an accomplice in some vile plot," but that is all he can expect from her until his "character be established by other means than [his] own assertions" (3:363). Mervyn does manage to remove the doubts of both Wortley and Mrs. Wentworth. Indeed, Wortley eventually comes to confide in Mervyn's "integrity . . . as much as he formerly suspected it," and he is won over, Mervyn writes, by his proper behavior (3:412). Yet the reader remains disturbed when he considers how much of the young man's reputation rests solely upon his own word and his innocent face.

The point of view of the novel helps to create in the reader's mind these doubts of Mervyn's true character, for we never see the events of the story directly. They are always filtered through the consciousness of one or another of the characters. The story is ostensibly told by Doctor Stevens, who introduces Mervyn and provides the frame in terms of which he recounts the incidents of his life. In addition, Mervyn's narrative includes a long digression supposedly spoken by Welbeck, who tells of his previous experience. Indeed, the point of view shifts from character to character until in the second part the device breaks down completely, and Mervyn simply writes the last episodes of the narrative. These stories within stories present some problems of interpretation. The reader is sometimes at several removes from the events being described and listening to a narrator—usually Mervyn—whose very purpose is to justify his acts to his friends. Only occasionally does another voice, like Wortley's, enter the dialogue, yet even when the testimony is damaging to the hero's character—and Mervyn's neighbors in the country level some serious charges against him—the strangely talkative young man simply explains them away with a plausible story that is accepted by his listeners.

It is probably true that in most—perhaps all—of these incidents, Mervyn is, as he claims, the victim of deceptive appearance, that things look damaging to his character which are not actually so. But if appearance is deceptive when others make adverse judgments upon him, how do we know it is not equally deceptive when Stevens and his wife resolve all doubts in his favor? Appearance alone is not to be trusted in either case, yet the doctor gives us little evidence on which to form an opinion of Mervyn's true nature. Other elements in the book illustrate clearly that appearance can be illusory. Welbeck himself had succeeded in deceiving the business community in Philadelphia simply by maintaining an imposing facade, and Mervyn had been duped by Welbeck's apparently sincere representations concerning the supposedly forged twenty thousand dollars that Mervyn destroyed. Thus, appearance has been much too deceptive in a considerable part of the novel for the reader to accept unreservedly the completely favorable judgment that Doctor Stevens makes on Arthur Mervyn's character.

This is not to say that Mervyn is a conscious fraud or that he deliberately lies when he tells the doctor the story of his life. His character is not that simple. Rather, Mervyn apparently thinks that he is being thoroughly honest when he informs us that his motives are pure, that his intentions are good, and that his only desire is to do good to others. Indeed, one can argue that his obvious sincerity is one of the most damaging elements in his character in that it seems to suggest a kind of self-deception on Mervyn's part that enables him to get what he wants materially out of life without cost either physically or emotionally to himself and allows him at the same time to preen himself on his own benevolence. He succeeds, but he apparently truly believes that he has done only good in the process. Certainly the contrast between his professions and his acts, between the ends he supposedly seeks and the ones he attains, suggests an interpretation of his sort. One may perhaps agree with Berthoff that we should not make too much of Brown as a conscious ironist in his treatment of Arthur Mervyn,[22] yet Berthoff's suggestion itself is provocative, for the development of the novel clearly reveals an irony that modern readers simply cannot ignore.

Not every critic agrees with this interpretation of *Arthur Mervyn.* Norman S. Grabo believes, for example, that Mervyn's "good fortune is not the result of connivance or self-seeking but that of basic honesty, a sense of justice, persistence in rectifying others' wrongs, and lots of good luck."[23] In support of his belief, he can point to a short piece, "Walstein's School of History," that appeared in the *Monthly Magazine* for September 1799.[24] Here Brown presents a theory of literature in which "fictitious memoirs" are composed "as models of human behavior," and he illustrates the point with a story, "Olivo Ronsica," which has long been recognized as a summary of part 1 of *Arthur Mervyn.* On the basis of this piece and his reading of the text, Grabo concludes that the novel—"at least through the first part"—is just the kind of story that Brown outlined to his brother the preceding February. In his treatment of the second part, Grabo sees a further connection with this piece. Mervyn goes on to develop "his sexual awareness," and in choosing his "profession and marriage partner," he embodies the relation of sex and property expressed in the magazine piece.[25]

No one will question the relation of "Olivo Ronsica" to the first part of *Arthur Mervyn,* but one may well doubt that the magazine piece provided Brown with a blueprint for the second part, little of which is mentioned in the story. One may doubt, too, the wisdom of turning outside the text to find a basis for its interpretation. Yet if one does so, he or she might better note the stress on deceptive appearance in both *Wieland* and *Ormond,* books that were written and published in the same span of time as *Arthur Mervyn.* Indeed, Thomas Craig, who precipitates the action in *Ormond,* is much like Arthur Mervyn in that he exhibits "a modest and ingenuous aspect" and tells so "circumstantial and consistent" a tale that its truth appears not to be doubted (2:7–8). It would be strange, indeed, if Brown, after writing so convincingly about deceptive appearances, should expect his readers to accept Arthur Mervyn at his own valuation, supported solely by his honest face and voluble tongue. In the first part of the novel, Brown may well have intended to write the kind of book that Grabo describes, but the change of direction that the story takes in part 2 surely indicates that Brown altered his purpose as he wrote.

For once, Brown's practice of improvisation may have worked to his advantage, for by the end of the second part, the character of Mervyn has become more complex and more interesting than the one Brown originally planned. Much of Mervyn's naiveté still remains, but as Brown composed part 2 of the novel, he developed new elements in the portrayal that make Mervyn a more realistic and believable—though certainly a less admirable—character than he had at first appeared to be. Beside him, such characters as Wieland and Ormond, well presented though they sometimes are, seem overly simple in development, and even Clara Wieland is much his inferior. All three at times tend to be overdrawn and lapse into the melodramatic. Yet, if Mervyn escapes the excesses that sometimes mar these characters, he also develops beyond the model of simple virtue that Brown had created in Constantia Dudley. Indeed, of all the characters discussed so far, only Carwin compares at all with Mervyn in his ability to justify his acts by rationalized motives, and even he lacks the subtlety and ambiguity that make the revelation of Mervyn's character so absorbing.

In other elements, too, *Arthur Mervyn* marks a departure from Brown's earlier work. In its emphasis upon the rise of its hero to a successful position in life and in the picture of both urban and rural society revealed in the process, the book comes closer in subject matter and technique to what might be called a modern novel than do his previous books.[26] In theme there are new developments too. Although some of the concepts—most notably that of deceptive appearance—are present here as they were in *Wieland* and *Ormond,* new ones are developed that show Brown's deep, continuing interest in moral and intellectual questions. Surely the emphasis that Arthur Mervyn places on his benevolent intent, especially throughout the second part of the novel, and the ends he manages to attain while professing benevolist principles suggest that Brown is raising serious doubts about the validity of such concepts as the sole guides to action. The effect of Mervyn's deeds is to call into question the principles he so glibly asserts, so that the book as a whole may legitimately be read as a strong counterstatement to the benevolist principles by which Mervyn claims to live.[27]

Yet, despite the well-drawn character of the hero and the intellectual interest that the novel generates, *Arthur Mervyn* is not a completely satisfactory book. It bears the signs of haste that mar all of Brown's novels, and it fails in a number of important qualities. The plot, especially in part 2, is a maze of incidents, and readers must work their way through a confusing series of events, not all of which are properly proportioned to the book's primary end. Thus, the novel as a whole lacks the clarity of structure that is apparent in at least the major parts of *Wieland* and *Ormond.* Much of the trouble derives from the point of view, for Brown did not handle successfully the stories within stories that make up so much of the book. In the hands of a Faulkner, the device can be effective,[28] but Brown was unable to carry it through to a successful conclusion. Except for the long digression by Welbeck, the technique works well enough in part 1, which has a roundness and completeness in its structure that is rather satisfying. In the second part, the first-person technique fails utterly to carry the story along, and the book becomes diffuse and confusing in its development. This method of telling his story was much too ambitious for Brown; he wrote too fast and revised too little to make it work.

Arthur Mervyn remains yet another of Brown's interesting and significant failures; with all its obvious faults in structure and presentation, it is a fascinating book. The setting of the novel has, at times, a reality seldom apparent in Brown's other books, and much of it serves a thematic purpose, at least in the first part. The scenes of the yellow fever in Philadelphia are drawn in convincing detail and serve as a meaningful contrast both to the rural countryside and to the more pleasant aspects of city life as represented by Doctor Stevens and the other virtuous men whom Mervyn learns of or encounters. All of these elements, however, are of but secondary importance to the character of Arthur Mervyn himself, whose climb to success is beautifully done. The recurring pattern of action revealed as Arthur moves between city and country, his attachment to women who seem able to provide him with material possessions, his relation to older men who can further his career, his willingness to be whatever the person who helps him wants him to become—all reveal the essential contradiction between his professed motives and his actual deeds that fixes his character unmistakably in the reader's mind. For all its faults, *Arthur Mervyn* remains a book well worth reading, if only because of the fine portrayal of Brown's most complex character.

Chapter Five
Edgar Huntly

In treating the two parts of *Arthur Mervyn* as a single novel, we have been forced to disregard the chronological order of Brown's works, for the second part of that book did not appear until over a year after the first. In this interval Brown engaged in a number of important activities. He launched his first periodical, the *Monthly Magazine and American Review,* in the spring of 1799 and published his fourth major novel, *Edgar Huntly; or, Memoirs of a Sleep-Walker.* Little is known about the composition of this book, but as Sydney J. Krause reconstructs it, Brown probably began work "some time after mid-February" 1799, and he had proceeded so far by April that he could publish an excerpt from it—"roughly Chapters 17 through 20"—in the April number of the *Monthly Magazine,* issued in May. By the middle of May, Brown left New York for Philadelphia, presumably to take the manuscript to Hugh Maxwell, who was to publish it, and to make arrangements for its publication. In the *Monthly Magazine* for July, the book is described as "now printing in Philadelphia." The first volume seems to have appeared in August and the entire book, issued in three volumes, toward the end of the year.[1]

It has long been known that in composing *Edgar Huntly,* Brown drew material from his unpublished novel, *Sky-Walk; or, The Man Unknown to Himself—an American Tale,* the first of his novels to be written.[2] This book, most probably completed in the spring of 1798,[3] was to have been published by James Watters in Philadelphia, and most of it had been printed before Watters died of the yellow fever in September. His executors would neither complete the printing nor release the sheets at a price that Brown or his friends could afford, and the book was subsequently lost. Drawing upon his memory, therefore, Brown used material from the lost novel when he wrote *Edgar Huntly* in 1799. From the comments of his friends on *Sky-Walk* and the excerpt from the book that appeared in the Philadelphia *Weekly Magazine* for 24 March 1798, Krause has argued that the novel centered on the phenomenon of sleepwalking, that the material from *Sky-Walk* was used primarily in the story of his life that Clithero Edny recounts in *Edgar Huntly,* and that, so far as can be determined, the earlier book did not deal with Indian warfare on the American frontier.[4]

The American Wilderness

By introducing such native material in *Edgar Huntly,* Brown made a real departure from his earlier work and set the stage for an aspect of American literature that was not to be fully developed for nearly a generation. Up to this time, most of Brown's best writing had been concerned with man in a civilized environment—a semirural one in *Wieland* and the city of Philadelphia in *Ormond* and in much of *Arthur Mervyn.* But in *Edgar Huntly,* Brown turned away from the social environments he had treated in those books to set the major events of his novel on the upper reaches of the Delaware River not far from the actual wilderness. Part of the action does take place in the settled rural district of Solebury, but the best episodes by far occur in Norwalk, a "rugged, picturesque and wild" area (4:19) of dense thickets, deep glens, rushing streams, and rocky hills that Huntly penetrates on several occasions. In this desolate area, he comes into open conflict with a band of hostile Indians and experiences frontier warfare in all its violence and brutality.

Such material had long been a staple of American writing in the many narratives of Indian captivity that had been popular since the seventeenth century. It appears as well in Ann Eliza Bleeker's *The History of Maria Kittle* (1793), often cited as the first American novel to include this material.[5] Brown's Indians bear a close resemblance to those in these books. With the exception of Old Deb, an aged woman who is shown to have some individual characteristics, the Indians in *Edgar Huntly* are stock figures of frontier narrative. Ruthless in warfare and cruel to their captives, they are dogged, determined foes who attack the settlements to kill and burn in cold blood. The settlers are equally fierce in their resistance. They yield no quarter in defense of their homes, and Huntly himself, though much averse to shedding blood, is forced to kill five Indians in the course of his adventure, finishing off the last, whom he had only wounded, with a bayonet. Such scenes of frontier violence illustrate Brown's attempt, as he notes in the preface (4:3), to turn the realities of American life to literary advantage.

More important, in view of the development that American literature was soon to undergo, is Brown's use of untouched nature as a major element in the novel. The most sharply drawn scenes in his earlier books had always been urban; the natural setting, when it was mentioned at all, served almost as a static—and not very interesting or important—backdrop to the action.

In *Edgar Huntly* the tangled wilderness of Norwalk, which plays so important a role in the novel, is described in some detail, and it is precisely the wildly romantic aspect of the area that is most stressed. Huntly is devoted, he writes, "to the spirit that breathes its inspiration in the gloom of forests and on the verge of streams," and he loves "to immerse [himself] in shades and dells, and hold converse with the solemnities and secrecies of nature in the rude retreats of Norwalk" (4:94–95). Such an attitude toward untouched nature had as yet found no expression in Brown's major fiction.[6] It marks a complete departure from the concepts expressed in his previous novels, and it points ahead to the use of the wilderness that we later find in the frontier romances of James Fenimore Cooper, whom Brown may well have influenced.[7]

To stress this aspect of the wilderness in *Edgar Huntly,* however, is to court the danger of distorting the meaning of the book. Warfel is surely right when he observes that Brown's success in "*Edgar Huntly* helped fix the setting of many American novels in the wilderness and lent impetus to the movement for picturing native scenery and native characters."[8] But it did much more. The setting is also important for the function it serves as the projection of the narrator's mind. Though Brown eschewed "puerile superstition and exploded manners; Gothic castles and chimeras" as materials for his novel (4:3), he did not abandon the Gothic as a mode of expression. We have already seen the use he made of enclosures in *Wieland* to symbolize the characters' minds. We should not be surprised, therefore, to find a cave serve the same function in *Edgar Huntly.* In a similar fashion, the bewildering paths by which Huntly traverses Norwalk in his compulsive pursuit of Clithero may be said to represent his mental wanderings. The tangled confusion of the untouched wilderness is thus an index to Huntly's mental state, just as the forest in some of Hawthorne's works symbolizes the moral state of such characters as Young Goodman Brown and Hester Prynne.[9]

Such a conclusion is certainly suggested in the early pages of the book, where a relationship is established between the hero's mind and the external scene. As the story begins, Huntly, alone and at nightfall, is walking home toward Solebury from a visit to his fiancée, Mary Waldegrave, who lives in another place and whose brother, Huntly's close friend, has recently been murdered. That Huntly must travel at night is of little concern to him. "A nocturnal journey in districts so romantic and wild," he writes, "was more congenial to my temper than a noon-day ramble," an opinion clearly evidenced in subsequent events. As night falls, Huntly's "sensations [sink] into melancholy," and, approaching the general area where the murder took place, he recalls "the insanity of vengeance and grief" (4:7) he had first experienced at his friend's death but from which he has since recovered. Nevertheless, his mind reverts to feelings of bitterness and revenge, and, as a result, he is driven compulsively to the site of Waldegrave's murder—a huge elm tree "on the verge of Norwalk"—though his path is along a different route (4:9). Huntly has thus turned out of his proper way to seek this isolated spot. In doing so, he triggers a series of events that eventually leads to his thrilling frontier adventures.

Psychological Development

At this point in the novel, Huntly, who narrates the tale himself in a long letter to Mary, is conscious of his mental aberration, and he is able to compare his first insane reactions at Waldegrave's death with his later recovery and relapse. Alert readers should thus be aware that in *Edgar Huntly* they face a problem of interpretation more difficult than that presented by either *Wieland* or *Arthur Mervyn.* The tale is told by a narrator in imminent danger of losing control over his mind and emotions, and readers are forced to look behind the episodes described to learn the real truth of the events. Once they know that Huntly is drawn to the tree by a strange compulsion which impels him to search the spot once again—he has already done it "an hundred times" (4:8)—for clues of the murderer, they should be on guard to question the motives and purposes that Huntly professes. If he slips once again into a mentally disturbed state, he will not be conscious of it himself, and they will have to perceive it through words and actions that to Huntly seem perfectly reasonable.

Edgar Huntly does indeed soon lapse into this unfortunate condition. As he approaches the elm tree where Waldegrave died, he sees a strange figure busily digging the earth beneath it and filling the air with sobs of grief. Huntly is at first deeply moved by the scene, but he soon reaches the conclusion—natural enough, perhaps, under the circumstances—that the stranger has had some connection with Waldegrave's death and that he need only make this man the object of his scrutiny to solve his friend's murder. This thought gives Huntly evident satisfaction because "it seemed as if the maze was no longer inscrutable. It would be quickly discovered who were the agents and instigators of" Waldegrave's murder (4:15). That Huntly has indeed been involved in an intellectual maze is obvious enough from the opening pages of the novel, but that his suspicions of the mysterious stranger and his desire to make him the object of his study are likely to lead him out of it must be questioned. He seems rather to be giving in to the strange compulsions that have heretofore moved him, and it is much more likely that his mental troubles will only be intensified by his actions.

The ensuing episodes clearly support this conclusion. Huntly eventually recognizes the stranger as Clithero Edny, a servant at Inglefield's, a nearby farm, but at this moment he merely perceives that the as-yet-unidentified man is walking in his sleep. Huntly observes that such a phenomenon denotes "a mind sorely wounded" and concludes that the man has perpetrated "some nefarious deed," most likely the murder of Waldegrave (4:13). Yet if the inability to sleep soundly indicates a deeply troubled mind, Huntly himself is in emotional difficulty, for he ponders so much on these matters that his own "slumbers were imperfect" (4:16). And the following night he returns to the elm tree to see if he can learn the truth from Clithero. He awaits his arrival for all of an hour when he suddenly perceives him there. This night, however, Clithero does not dig but muses for a while and then bursts forth "into sighs and lamentations." When Clithero rises to go, Huntly determines "to tread, as closely as possible, in his footsteps," and he pursues him first "along an obscure path" and then "through a most perplexing undergrowth of bushes and briars" (4:18). The action of neither man is normal, and one is certainly justified in reading a symbolic meaning into such strange behavior.

Seen in this light, the journey of Huntly into the region of Norwalk bespeaks the developing madness in a man who has left his normal path to satisfy his irrational compulsions. Clithero leads the way through a difficult labyrinth, hurries along the verge of a precipice, descends into a valley, and eventually buries himself in a cave. Later we learn that the cavern has often served Clithero as a place to brood over his sorrows (4:89) so that it comes to be the symbol of a mind possessed, but even without this clue to its interpretation, we could still recognize the cave as the external expression of an obsessive mental state and the journey into the wilderness as movement through an intellectual labyrinth that can only terminate in such a place.[10] Huntly's mad pursuit of Clithero thus provides a clear indication of his unbalanced mind. Indeed, he realizes himself that his mad career had taken him through "a maze, oblique, circuitous," in which "all dangers were overlooked, and all difficulties defied. I plunged into obscurities, and clambered over obstacles, from which, in a different state of mind, and with a different object of pursuit, I should have recoiled with invincible timidity" (4:23). Nonetheless, he continues his mad career. Driven, like other of Brown's characters, by an obsessive desire to know, he is determined to learn the reasons for Clithero's strange behavior.

The truth turns out to be something quite different from what he had expected. Convinced that Clithero is the murderer of Waldegrave, Huntly confronts him with his suspicions. Huntly is certain that he has drawn just inferences from the events he has observed and is filled with benevolent feelings that he can lead the unfortunate man back to virtue. In this state of mind, he resembles both the characters in *Wieland,* who believe they can arrive at truth through the interpretation of sensory evidence, and the benevolent-minded Arthur Mervyn, who is always sure his motives are good even when he is pursuing selfish ends. Like all of these other characters, Huntly is shown to be in error in the inference he has made and in his belief that benevolent feelings are sufficient to lead him to proper goals. Indeed, Clithero informs him of his errors at once. "The inferences which you have drawn, with regard to my designs, and my conduct," Clithero tells him, "are a tissue of destructive errors. You, like others, are blind to the most momentous consequences of your actions." Although Huntly had intended to do him good, his "misguided zeal, and random efforts," Clithero argues, will do him harm instead (4:35–36).

To illustrate his contention, Clithero, in a long digression, relates the story of his life. The son of Irish peasants, he had attracted the attention of a widow, Mrs. Lorimer, who took him into her household, educated him, and made him the companion of her son. Although he and the son soon part company because of Clithero's somewhat censorious criticism of his behavior, he is retained in Mrs. Lorimer's family in a position of trust and becomes engaged to Clarice, his patroness's niece. This girl is the daughter of Arthur Wiatte, Mrs. Lorimer's twin brother, who, although still retaining his sister's deep affection, is described as so utterly depraved as to be a remorseless villain. He has hurt his sister deeply by managing to drive away her lover, Sarsefield, and by urging their parents to marry her to another. After the parents' deaths, he wastes the patrimony and eventually becomes a highwayman. When he is sentenced to be transported for his crimes, his sister refuses to intercede on his behalf, for she knows that his vice is incurable and that this punishment is the most lenient he can expect. Wiatte is thought to have died in a mutiny aboard the ship in which he sailed, but Mrs. Lorimer, under the delusion that their lives must end together, continues to believe that he is still alive. Meanwhile, Sarsefield, who has spent many years in India and America, returns to renew his acquaintance with the family.

At this point, Wiatte once again appears upon the scene and precipitates Clithero's tragedy. Returning one evening from delivering a sum of money to a banker, Clithero is walking through a dark lane when a man steps to his side, fires a shot that grazes his forehead, and draws a knife to kill him. By a kind of reflex action, Clithero, on seeing the glint of the knife, draws a pistol and fires, mortally wounding his assailant. Clithero does not know who his attacker is, and Brown has arranged the incident in such a way that no guilt can be assigned to Clithero in preserving his own life. Some of the people who rush to the scene know him, the case is easily explained, and Clithero is allowed to go on his way unchallenged. When the assailant is carried out of the lane and into the light, Clithero immediately recognizes him as Mrs. Lorimer's brother. This recognition sets Clithero's mind off on a line of thought that leads to appalling consequences. Understandably upset by what has happened, Clithero loses his power of clear thought and reasonable action. In a kind of mental stupor, he wanders back unconsciously almost to the banker's door; but, more important, strange thoughts arise in his mind to torment him.

He begins to think how the knowledge of Wiatte's death will afflict Mrs. Lorimer, who not only wishes her brother no harm but also believes that she must die when he does. Clithero madly reproaches himself for what he has done and actually thinks himself an ingrate because he has purchased his life at the price of her sorrow. "My fancy began to be infected with the errors of my understanding," he states. "The mood into which my mind was plunged was incapable of any propitious intermission. All within me was tempestuous and dark" (4:78). He begins to think that perhaps Mrs. Lorimer is already dead, and he rushes to her room to test the truth of his fears. But even the sound of her steady breathing fails to calm him, for he begins to fear what she will suffer when she wakes to learn the truth, and he actually resolves to kill her himself to protect her from that knowledge. At the point of striking her with a dagger, however, he hears a shriek behind him; Mrs. Lorimer herself diverts the blade; and Clithero learns that he has almost stabbed Clarice, who is in her aunt's bed. Mrs. Lorimer faints away on hearing of her brother's death, and, convinced that she is dead, Clithero flees the house, eventually to make his way to America.

Having disburdened himself of his story, Clithero disappears into the wilderness and leaves Huntly alone to muse on his tale. Huntly is fascinated by the story, both because it involves Sarsefield—who, we learn, had become his friend and mentor while he was in America—and because of the nature of the tale itself. But instead of convincing him that his inferences are erroneous and his benevolent feelings misdirected, as Clithero had evidently expected, it seems rather to confirm him in error. Though he realizes his suspicions were wrong, he interprets Clithero's conduct as "an act of momentary insanity" originating in a "spirit of mistaken benevolence" and considers it "the fruit of an ardent and grateful spirit" (4:90–91). Huntly argues that Clithero is really blameless, not only in his killing of Wiatte but also in his attempted murder of Mrs. Lorimer, for, in his opinion, Clithero "desired to confer on her the highest and the only benefit of which he believed her capable. He sought to rescue her from tormenting regrets and lingering agonies" (4:110). His defense of Clithero is not simply that the servant was insane at the time of his act but that his intent was benevolent. The reader is thus clearly warned that Huntly's own benevolent purposes may be equally mad and lead to similarly disastrous results.

Descent into Madness

Huntly does not realize that his acts are anything but rational. As obsessed now with the idea that he must help the unfortunate Clithero as he had previously been with seeking Waldegrave's murderer, Huntly determines to follow Clithero into the wilderness, though he realizes it is unlikely that he will be able to locate him there. Thus, once again following Clithero's lead, Huntly plunges into the labyrinth that Clithero has repeatedly threaded and penetrates the cave where he has brooded over the past. Relentless in his pursuit, Huntly makes his way through the cavern to an isolated peak in the wilderness and actually finds Clithero sitting on the far side of a deep chasm in a position that seems totally inaccessible. Determined that his benevolent intention to restore Clithero to sanity shall not be frustrated, Huntly makes repeated trips between the farm and Norwalk. He fells a tree across the chasm so that he can approach the spot where he saw Clithero, and he even leaves food where he thinks he will find it. Aware as we are of Clithero's madness, we can interpret Huntly's pursuit of him into Norwalk only as an objective projection of Huntly's own descent on the same path to insanity.

Like Arthur Mervyn, Edgar Huntly engages in strangely compulsive actions, which he justifies to himself as purely benevolent. As time goes on, we increasingly recognize how far from normality his actions really are. Impelled by his strong curiosity, Huntly pries relentlessly into Clithero's past. He examines the locked box that Clithero had left at Inglefield's farm and works on it until he releases the hidden spring that opens it. Though he finds nothing of interest inside, he learns to his consternation that he cannot close it again—a symbol, perhaps, of his inability to foresee or control the consequences of his acts. He even digs beneath the elm tree where he had first seen Clithero walking in his sleep and turns up another locked box buried beneath the turf. On his return to Inglefield's that same night, Huntly is surprised to discover that Clithero has come back, destroyed the box whose secrecy Huntly had violated, and disappeared again. But even this knowledge does not deter Huntly from smashing the box that he has just dug up or from reading the manuscript, written by Mrs. Lorimer and defending her actions in regard to her brother, that Clithero had concealed in it.

So far down the path of irrational action has Huntly gone that he even begins to act like Clithero himself. Just as the unfortunate servant has preserved Mrs. Lorimer's manuscript, so also has Huntly kept a package of letters written by his murdered friend. Both take extraordinary steps to preserve their papers, and both unconsciously hide them while walking in their sleep. Indeed, both have feelings of guilt regarding the authors of the manuscripts. Clithero, of course, thinks he has caused his patroness's death; Huntly, that he has failed to fulfill his friend's wishes. Huntly's belief is revealed in a strange dream that he has one night. "During my sleep," he writes, "the image of Waldegrave flitted before me. Methought the sentiment that impelled him to visit me, was not affection or complacency, but inquietude and anger. Some service or duty remained to be performed by me, which I had culpably neglected: to inspirit my zeal, to awaken my remembrance, and incite me to the performance of this duty, did this glimmering messenger, this half indignant apparition, come" (4:130). The dream is powerful enough to disturb his sleep because he awakes long before his accustomed hour and thinks immediately of his manuscripts.

These letters are the cause of his guilty feelings, for most of them were written by Waldegrave during a period of irreligious thought when he attempted to persuade Huntly to accept his new intellectual views. Because Waldegrave later changed his mind and, in a series of conversations, tried to influence Huntly to return to religious belief, Waldegrave had pleaded with his friend to destroy the letters lest they lead someone astray. Huntly still remains somewhat influenced by the arguments that the letters contain, and, unwilling to part with any remembrance of his friend's active mind, he has failed to comply with his request. Worse, he has even promised Mary, albeit reluctantly, to send her copies of her brother's letters, and he now begins to fear that, by fulfilling his promise to her, he might make the dead Waldegrave the unwilling cause of his sister's apostasy. On awaking from his strange dream, Huntly thinks these matters over and finally decides to send her only the sections which might be considered safe for her to read. When he goes to the cabinet to get the letters, however, he is aghast to find them missing.

Their disappearance is completely inexplicable to him: no one but Mary knows of their existence, and he has kept them locked in a cabinet as cunningly contrived as Clithero's box. The key to the cabinet is always kept in a locked box, and the drawer within the cabinet, where the manuscripts are deposited, can only be opened, like Clithero's box, by a secret spring. Utterly at a loss to explain what has happened, Huntly is struggling with his problem when his uncle knocks at the door to ask why he has been acting so strangely during the night; he thinks he has heard him pacing back and forth on the top story of the house. It does not occur to either of them that Huntly has begun to sleepwalk, and it is not until the end of the novel that the full truth is revealed. Huntly and Clithero have acted in precisely the same manner. While still asleep, Clithero had removed his manuscript from his trick box and buried it under the elm tree. In a similar fashion, impelled by his feelings of guilt at not having obeyed his friend's injunction, Huntly arises after his dream, performs while still asleep the complicated process of opening his cabinet, and conceals his manuscripts "between the rafters and shingles of" his uncle's roof (4:260, 278).

Thus driven by fears and compulsions into acts that parallel those of the mad Clithero, Huntly is rapidly losing complete control of his actions and needs only one additional shock to push him completely over the line into madness. That shock comes almost immediately. Although anxious to seek out Clithero in the wilderness once again, Huntly decides to remain at home the following night to recoup his strength. While sitting alone in the parlor, he is visited by a stranger who brings distressing news. The visitor, named Weymouth, had been a friend of Waldegrave;[11] and, while on a speculative voyage to Europe to engage in trade, he had consigned a large sum of money to Waldegrave for safekeeping before his return home. Shipwrecked off the coast of Portugal on his homeward voyage, Weymouth had been long delayed, only to learn on his arrival that Waldegrave was dead. Unable to locate any relatives, he is directed to Edgar Huntly as the man who might know of Waldegrave's affairs. Huntly had indeed found a large sum of money in Waldegrave's estate, a sum that neither he nor Mary could explain since Waldegrave's occupation, the teaching of Negroes, paid him only subsistence. Because they could find no papers concerning the source of the money, they felt justified, after an interval, in using it for Mary's support.

Huntly is shocked to learn that the rightful owner of the money has appeared. An honest man, he will, of course, see to it that the money is returned, but this act will entail a complete change in his and Mary's plans. Since his parents' deaths at the hands of Indians, Huntly and his sisters have been totally dependent on their uncle, whose son, we learn, hates them so much that he will probably turn them out when the farm comes into his hands. Because Huntly has no means to support a wife, he and Mary had expected to live on the money Waldegrave had left, and, after his marriage to Mary, Huntly had planned to provide a refuge in their home for his sisters. Weymouth's arrival, therefore, is a crushing blow to these hopes. Coming on top of his loss of Waldegrave's letters, his feelings of guilt at having preserved them, and his compulsive desire to help Clithero, whom he has in effect driven into the wilderness by prying into his past, this revelation finally forces Huntly over the edge of sanity—a fact revealed in one of the most startling turns of plot to be found in an American novel.

Edgar Huntly abruptly changes direction at this point. The ensuing chapter opens with Huntly in complete darkness, his body aching, and his mind completely disoriented. He does not know where he is or how he got there, and only gradually does he acquire an understanding of his surroundings. It is obvious to the reader that Huntly is trapped in the cave. He has, if one may take the action figuratively, not only followed Clithero over the bounds of sanity but has also suffered a kind of symbolic death—the first of several that he may be said to experience in the novel.[12] In a passage that reminds one of some of Poe's short tales and of *The Narrative of Arthur Gordon Pym,*[13] Huntly describes his condition: "Sometimes I imagined myself buried alive. Methought I had fallen into seeming death and my friends had consigned me to the tomb, from which a resurrection was impossible." Such a thought does not terrify him since, he goes on to say, "my state was full of tumult and confusion, and my attention was incessantly divided between my painful sensations and my feverish dreams." Huntly's mind is, at this time, in a "species of delerium." He exists, "as it were in a wakeful dream" in which "the images of the past occurred in capricious combinations, and vivid hues" (4:161–62).

Return to Sanity

Huntly's recovery is only gradual, and his return to sanity is not complete until the end of the book. Slowly, however, he does reorient himself to the physical world. When he first awoke, he writes, his "thoughts were wildering and mazy, and though consciousness were present, it was disconnected with the loco-motive or voluntary power" (4:159). But he eventually perceives that his posture is supine, and gradually he rises and feels his way around his prison. Still disoriented, he can locate himself in neither space nor time: "the utter darkness disabled me from comparing directions and distances" (4:161), and he was excluded from measuring time by his inability to perceive change in the external world and by his incapacity to gauge it accurately through "the succession of [his] thoughts" (4:162). The cravings of hunger enable him to focus his thinking more sharply; he then attempts to locate himself by sound, succeeding at last in identifying his position by the echoes he generates, which resemble, "with remarkable exactness" (4:163), the sounds he had previously produced in the cave. Now fully aware of his precise location, Huntly begins to think rationally of his predicament and to recognize that he has by some mischance fallen into a pit in the cavern. Properly oriented again in space, he attempts to extricate himself from his difficulties.

The rest of the book describes Huntly's struggle to return to normality, but the process is long and difficult and beset with numerous unforeseen dangers that teach him how little he knows about his own strengths and weaknesses. Slowly and with great effort, he makes his way up the sides of the pit, frequently falling back again when the walls become too smooth, but at last he draws himself painfully over the brink. No sooner does he arrive at relative safety than he sees two spots of light gleaming in the darkness, spots he immediately recognizes as the eyes of a panther. Fortunately he has a tomahawk, which, with the unexpected strength called forth by the desperateness of his situation, he flings at the animal. Recovering from the sinking reaction he immediately experiences, he feels such pangs of hunger that he feeds on the carcass of the beast he has killed. So avidly does he eat that he falls victim to excruciating agonies in his stomach. At length, his pains subside, and he falls into a deep sleep but is disturbed by dreams of tantalizing visions of food and drink that he cannot approach. He awakes less feeble of body, having survived the natural dangers that have assailed him.

In the succeeding action, Huntly encounters new perils; these derive not so much from the physical environment as from human passions and errors. To be sure, he awakes with a burning thirst, but as he works his way toward the entrance of the cave, he hears running water with which to assuage it. What keeps him from rushing to it is the recognition that a number of Indians are encamped in the mouth of the cavern, whose warlike intent is revealed by the presence of a female captive. In a suspenseful series of incidents, Huntly manages to escape from the cave, and, driven by his great thirst, to overcome his aversion to bloodshed and his childhood fear of Indians derived from his parents' massacre. He kills one of them and even succeeds in making off with the unfortunate captive. His escape from the remaining savages is only temporary; after eating and resting at an abandoned hut in the wilderness, he encounters them again and eventually kills them all. Edgar Huntly thus discovers within himself unforeseen and unexpected resources when his very survival depends upon action, but he also learns that physical weakness can betray him. Approached by a party of whites in pursuit of the savages, Huntly, who had been so strong and capable when danger was imminent, faints away when help arrives. His swoon is mistaken for death,[14] and Huntly revives only to find himself abandoned in the wilderness.

His mind, moreover, continues to play him false, for, confronted with certain specific facts, he leaps, as he has done before, to erroneous conclusions. On his escape from the cave, Huntly had hurriedly seized the musket of one of the Indians, but he had had no chance to examine it closely until he arrived at the hut. He is horrified to learn, when he does inspect it, that the musket is his own, the very one given him by Sarsefield and left in the closet of his chamber at his uncle's house. He concludes that his "uncle and . . . sisters had been murdered; the dwelling had been pillaged, and this had been a part of the plunder" (4:185). Such thoughts of an imagined catastrophe had almost driven him back to the mountain to slaughter the remaining Indians he had left there, a mad intent that is thwarted only by their timely arrival at the hut and their subsequent destruction at Huntly's hands. When he awakes from his swoon and finds himself once more alone, he struggles back toward Solebury, burning with impatience to learn what has become of his family (4:213).

Huntly is thus as driven by compulsion to make his way home as he had been to seek Waldegrave's murderer or to pursue Clithero in order to help him, and his imprudence almost leads to his destruction. Refreshed at a frontier cabin, he attempts to hurry over a dangerous ridge. He soon loses his way as night is falling. Unable to sleep or to make a fire to protect himself from the icy wind that rises, he contemplates leaping into the river that flows below the cliff, for, once in the water, he could seek a road along the bank and make his way home. As he prepares to leap, he hears the sound of human voices, and his fears convince him that Indians are once again near. Lying quietly on the ground, he sees seven figures pass in the darkness, but an eighth, coming behind the rest, stops and looks toward him. Fearful that an Indian could not fail to perceive him even in the darkness, Huntly jumps to his feet, fires his piece at the shadowy figure, and, dropping the musket, leaps into the water. There he is barely missed by the bullets fired after his fleeing figure.[15] Huntly survives his brush with death and eventually makes his way along the opposite shore, where new evidence supports his conviction that his family has been destroyed.

When he approaches a ford in the river, he meets a country man who informs him of recent events: that Indians had attacked the settlements "and that one house in Solebury had been rifled and burnt on the night before the last." Such information only adds fuel to Huntly's fears, and since the man does not remember whose house it was, Huntly's imagination runs riot. "All was lost," he writes; "all for whose sake I desired to live, had perished by the hands of these assassins. That dear home, the scene of my sportive childhood, of my studies, labours and recreations, was ravaged by fire and the sword: was reduced to a frightful ruin." He fears that "the means of subsistence itself" are lost to him by the death of his uncle and by the succession of his cousin to the farm, and he laments the loss of his books and possessions. He is comforted to hear that one of the girls who had been captured by the Indians has been recovered and immediately believes that this refers to one of his sisters; he completely forgets that he had himself rescued a captive who was no relation to him (4:234–35). So much have fear, fatigue, and the memory of his parents' tragedy affected him that he is incapable of thinking calmly; instead, he rushes madly on his compulsive way.

Huntly is eventually disabused of his wild errors. Entering a house to seek information and help, he runs unexpectedly into his own packet of Waldegrave's letters and finally into Sarsefield himself, who has arrived in America, visited the Huntly farm, and, realizing what Huntly has done, located the letters hidden under the roof. Sarsefield informs him that his uncle is in fact dead, killed by an Indian who had taken the musket with which the uncle had armed himself in going out on the expedition, but the farm and Edgar's sisters are completely safe. Huntly learns that his precipitate action had delayed his own rescue and placed his and Sarsefield's lives in danger, for, in leaving the hut where he had fainted, he had missed Sarsefield, who later came in search of him and found him gone. And in firing on the imagined Indian on the ridge, he had almost killed his friend, who had likewise almost killed him when he leaped from the cliff. Indeed, Sarsefield himself had twice given Huntly up for dead. Thus, Brown seems to say, are human plans thwarted by chance and circumstances, some external and physical, but others residing in the human being himself, like the fears and compulsions by which Huntly has been madly driven.

Edgar Huntly should realize at this point that his plans and purposes, his desire to do good for others, should be viewed with considerable caution, since so many of his inferences have been proved false and so much of his supposedly benevolent action has led to near disaster for himself and others. He comes to believe, as he writes to Mary, that "the mass of misery and error" in which man is "forever involved" is made "by his own hands," and he recognizes how mental phantoms had led him to the cave in his sleep and dropped him into the pit. "How little cognizance have men," he concludes, "over the actions and motives of each other! How total is our blindness with regard to our own performances!" (4:278). These words echo a statement Huntly made at the beginning of his narrative: "What light has burst upon my ignorance of myself and of mankind! How sudden and enormous the transition from uncertainty to knowledge!" (4:6). The passages serve as a kind of envelope for his long letter to Mary, and if the book ended with that account, we could only conclude that Huntly has achieved self-knowledge from his experience.

But the book does not end here. Brown appends three letters, two from Huntly to Sarsefield, and a reply from his mentor, who is given the final word in the book. These reveal that Huntly's enlightenment is not so complete as it seemed to him to be. Despite his apparent awareness of human capacity for self-deception and error, particularly in ascertaining the motives of others and in foreseeing the consequences of his own acts, he persists in his desire to help Clithero, even though it was this very purpose which had first led him into the difficulties that he has just barely survived. He still believes that he has judged him correctly and has it within his power to bring him back to normality. Thus, when Clithero is brought in wounded after having been rescued from Indian captivity, Huntly tries to enlist Sarsefield to help the injured man. Sarsefield, of course, will have nothing to do with him and even withholds the medical aid that he could dispense. But at Huntly's insistence, he does reluctantly agree that the young man should tell Clithero that he did not kill Mrs. Lorimer, now Sarsefield's wife, even though Sarsefield does not believe that Clithero's insanity can be cured.

Before Huntly can accomplish his purpose, Clithero again escapes to the wilderness, and Huntly pursues him once more in the belief that he can "afford him comfort, and inspire him with courage and hope" (4:284). He finds him at Old Deb's hut, and although the scowling Clithero tries to withdraw from him, Huntly persists, confident in the belief that in telling him the truth—that Mrs. Sarsefield is alive and well in New York—he may relieve him of his feelings of guilt and remorse. In an act of remarkable imprudence, Huntly reveals not only these facts but the house where she lives, and he is horrified at Clithero's response: "I will fly to the spot which thou describest. I will ascertain thy falsehood with my own eyes. If she be alive then am I reserved for the performance of a new crime. My evil destiny will have it so. If she be dead, I shall make *thee* expiate" (4:289). Too late, Huntly realizes that Clithero is indeed a maniac who cannot be recalled to sanity by any power that Huntly possesses. All he can do is to dispatch a letter to New York telling Sarsefield what has happened and urging him to head Clithero off.

Huntly's defense of his actions is significant, for it clearly reveals how seriously he has erred in trusting without question his ability to draw just inferences from events and in acting upon those conclusions. "Yet who could foresee this consequence of my intelligence?" Huntly writes to Sarsefield. "I imagined, that Clithero was merely a victim of erroneous gratitude, a slave of the errors of his education, and the prejudices of his rank, that his understanding was deluded by phantoms in the mask of virtue and duty, and not as you have strenuously maintained, utterly subverted." Huntly knows that his actions must be censured, for he admits that his "unfortunate temerity has created this evil." Nonetheless, he defends himself with the thought that, although he has erred, he did so "not through sinister or malignant intentions, but from the impulse of misguided, indeed, but powerful benevolence" (4:290). His "benevolence" has consequences that are not revealed until Sarsefield's reply. Clithero has indeed been intercepted, but the terror that Sarsefield's wife experienced on learning that he was approaching caused her to miscarry, and Clithero ended his life a suicide.

The novel concludes, therefore, with Huntly fully aware, presumably, of the consequences of his actions. He has been made to see his madness for what it is and to admit the errors into which he has fallen. Yet despite these facts, *Edgar Huntly* does not come to a point of repose. The final letters clearly reveal that the young man is capable of self-deception even after attaining a high degree of insight into his problem. He ignores the advice of his mentor—the man on whom he must depend for his livelihood—and plunges once again into the maze from which he has just extricated himself. In the light of this evidence, one may well question if Huntly has really achieved the enlightenment he needs or whether, given sufficient provocation, he will fall once more into similar errors. His situation is certainly awkward. He confronts a Sarsefield, who, justifiably upset by what he has done, rebukes him in no uncertain terms, and Brown gives no hint of an eventual reconciliation between the two men. The conclusion of the novel finds them at an impasse, with Huntly facing a future that is at best problematic.

Thematic Meaning and Literary Value

In this respect, Edgar Huntly resembles Clara Wieland, for both characters undergo harrowing experiences, projected through the Gothic elements in the novels, and both, though apparently cured of their madness by their association with rationalist mentors, still show some signs of their delusion at the end. Like Theodore Wieland, too, Huntly has fallen under the influence of such strong irrational forces that he is incapable of estimating his own mental state.[16] His friendship with Waldegrave and his desire to avenge his friend's death disqualify him as an objective seeker of truth in trying to determine the identity of his murderer, and his abnormal mental condition, paralleling that of the mad Clithero, makes him an unsuitable judge of that unfortunate man. The series of emotional shocks he receives in the course of the narrative and the severe physical and mental strain he undergoes on his return from the cave further affect his ability to think rationally. While the events are taking place, Huntly himself is scarcely aware of his own deficiency, but relying to the end on his own disturbed mind, he continues to act in the world as if he were in complete control of his reason and were able to foresee clearly the results of the chain of circumstances that he sets in motion.

But if Brown in *Edgar Huntly* echoes the critique of the rationalist approach to life that he had made in *Wieland,* he also questions the validity of the emotionalist attitude that Huntly sometimes exhibits. For, although Edgar Huntly believes that Clithero's madness can be cured by the use of reason and the simple statement of the truth that his patroness is not dead (4:95, 285–86), he also feels a powerful sympathy for the man. He observes at one point in the novel that, should his arguments fail, there are other means by which he might manage to help him. Thus, he writes that "to set by him in silence, to moisten his hand with tears, to sigh in unison, to offer him the spectacle of sympathy, the solace of believing that his demerits were not estimated by so rigid a standard by others as by himself, that one at least among his fellow men regarded him with love and pity, could not fail to be of benign influence" (4:106). Though Huntly's own madness and subsequent personal troubles keep him from fulfilling this purpose, it is with similarly benevolent intent that he finally seeks Clithero out in Norwalk to reveal the presence of Sarsefield's wife in America, with the disastrous results that ensue.

Huntly's appeal to benevolent motives in extenuation of his acts reinforces the critique of benevolist principles that had already appeared in other of Brown's novels. One is reminded of the characters who sought to explain their deeds by similar means: Carwin, who argued at one point that in projecting his voice he was conferring a benefit on the Wielands when in reality he had merely succumbed to his overpowering curiosity and desire to meddle in their affairs; and Ormond, who had used the same plea in his attempt to justify the murder of Stephen Dudley. More closely allied to the view as it appears in *Edgar Huntly,* however, are Arthur Mervyn's professions of benevolent intent at the very moment his actions are helping him toward selfish ends. Since this aspect of his character becomes clearer in the second part of *Arthur Mervyn,* it is possible that the treatment of benevolence in *Edgar Huntly,* written between the two parts of the other book, may well have influenced the development of Mervyn's character and even caused the sharp change of direction that Brown made in composing the second part of his novel.

Be that as it may, Brown makes no attempt to resolve the philosophic questions he raises in *Edgar Huntly.* Reason, as embodied in the advice of the level-headed Sarsefield, seems inadequate to divert the young man from his compulsive acts, for the psychological forces at work on him are overwhelming. Sympathy and benevolent feeling are also unavailing, for they lead only to disaster. Brown presents no alternative values for those Huntly professes. He does reveal that Huntly still retains, in part at least, the irreligious views that Waldegrave unfortunately instilled in him (4:133), but little is made of Huntly's disbelief, and there is not even the suggestion that his philosophic position contributes to his irrational behavior.[17] We cannot conclude, as we could with *Ormond,* that Brown affirms the importance of religious belief as the guide to life. We can merely observe that in *Edgar Huntly,* Brown, as he did in *Arthur Mervyn,* allows his protagonist to play out the intellectual drama in which he is involved and to suggest through the obvious contrast between the principles he professes and the results he achieves in acting upon them the serious reservations that Brown himself had apparently developed concerning their validity.

Although the reader might wish that the book were intellectually more rounded and complete, one may still accept it as an effectively written work of fiction. Admittedly there are flaws. A number of loose ends are left at the end of the book. No provision is made for Huntly's sisters. They are staying at Inglefield's farm when Huntly goes for the last time in search of Clithero, but no further mention is made of them. We do not learn what happens to Mary Waldegrave, whether she and Huntly ever marry or what they will live on if they do, for the question of Weymouth's claim is also left unsettled. Brown may have done all this deliberately, for Huntly's fate is also undecided as the book ends. But given Brown's method of writing, it is much more likely that he neglected to tidy up the details. Flaws like these seem more significant, however, when the reader reflects on the book than they appear to be when hurried along by the suspenseful action, and one is inclined to discount their importance in the final judgment because of the obvious strengths the novel also exhibits.

Foremost among them are the striking effects that Brown creates in the book. Few readers, one may suppose, can easily forget such impressive scenes as that in which Huntly first sees Clithero digging under the elm, or that in the cave in which Huntly—like Poe's protagonist in "The Pit and the Pendulum"[18]—returns to consciousness and reorients himself to his physical surroundings. Brown was surely as adept as Poe in creating the kind of mood that was to characterize the work of his great successor.[19] But as with Poe, there is more to Brown's use of the setting than the creation of mood. The maze or labyrinth through which Huntly makes his way across Norwalk, the cave he enters and the pit into which he falls, his struggle to return to Solebury, and his symbolic deaths and rebirths are all the outward projections of his inner state. In his skillful use of devices like these, Brown points ahead to the similar works of Poe and Hawthorne. Seen in these terms, *Edgar Huntly,* like *Wieland,* foreshadows a whole series of American tales and romances that project through the Gothic mode the psychological state of the characters.

Noteworthy too is Brown's use of the double, a literary device that came into prominence around the time he was writing. Although Brown most probably did not know the German authors who used the technique, it is obvious from the book that he intended Clithero Edny to serve as Edgar Huntly's doppelgänger, or second self. Both are sleepwalkers, both conceal manuscripts in cunningly contrived cases and secrete them while walking in their sleep, both withdraw into the wilderness of Norwalk and retreat into a cave, a symbol of their innermost selves. By this means Brown is able to show that Huntly's is a divided psyche in conflict with itself and that, in following Clithero into the labyrinth of Norwalk, he is in pursuit of a self that he perceives as other. Arising from his own sense of guilt, the double is a second self with whom he identifies and to whom he is irresistibly drawn.[20] In using this device, Brown once again foreshadows the work of subsequent American writers: Poe, for example, who employs the technique in a number of his tales, but most especially "William Wilson," and James, who, a century later, would use it in "The Jolly Corner."

The forward-looking aspects of *Edgar Huntly*—Brown's use of Indian warfare in the wilderness and the psychological double in a Gothic landscape—are enough to secure its place in American literary history, but emphasis on them must not be allowed to obscure the intrinsic value of the book and its place in the Brown canon. *Edgar Huntly* is closely related to two other of Brown's novels. Like *Arthur Mervyn* it is the story of a young man who professes to act from motives of benevolence but who can always find good reasons for doing what he seems compelled to do. Both are interesting characters, for Huntly and Mervyn are men unknown to themselves. But if Mervyn can skate on the surface of life and always succeed, Huntly is driven to the inner reaches of his mind and is made to face the disaster his acts have caused. There is less ambiguity about his character and the meaning of his experience. More deeply symbolic than *Arthur Mervyn, Edgar Huntly* is the better book. The plot line is straighter, the point of view more consistent, the theme more profound, and the whole better focused than the rather confused and chaotic *Arthur Mervyn*.

Edgar Huntly also resembles *Wieland* in that both make use of Gothic elements to reveal the psychological aberrations of the principal characters, but it marks an advance on the earlier book in that it places the locus of Gothic terror in the American wilderness. Nothing in *Wieland* surpasses those incidents in which Huntly struggles to return from the cave. Yet taken on balance, *Edgar Huntly* is not the equal of *Wieland* in a number of critical areas. Except for the mishandled subplot, Brown's first novel is more sharply focused. Clithero's long account of his life and Weymouth's digression midway through *Edgar Huntly* detract from the tone of the novel, and the book does not match the Gothic intensity of *Wieland* until Huntly's encounters in the wilderness. Indeed, one may even argue the superiority of *Wieland* in its breadth of thematic development, for, unlike the later book, it reveals its meaning through a number of different characters who play variations upon it without detracting from the central interest that is focused on Clara. In plot construction, consistency of tone, and thematic development, therefore, *Edgar Huntly* falls somewhat short of *Wieland,* which, despite its faults, is Brown's most successful novel.

Chapter Six
Minor Novels

When *Edgar Huntly* began to appear in the summer of 1799, Brown had completed a remarkable year as an author. Most of the work on which his literary reputation depends had been published within the preceding twelve months. Of his major novels, only part 2 of *Arthur Mervyn* lay in the future. Brown was never again to write so prolifically or so well, but his career as a novelist was by no means over. In addition to the second part of *Arthur Mervyn, Clara Howard* and *Jane Talbot* were still to come from his pen, novels hardly the equal of the work he had already done but still worth close attention. He had also begun to publish a substantial and important fragment, *Memoirs of Stephen Calvert.* This book began to appear in the *Monthly Magazine and American Review* in June 1799, around the time he was finishing *Edgar Huntly,* and continued in installments until June 1800, close to the time the second part of *Arthur Mervyn* must have been completed. Brown's final novels, *Clara Howard* and *Jane Talbot,* two books written in the sentimental manner, did not appear until 1801.

Stephen Calvert

Brown had begun to write *Stephen Calvert* in late August or early September 1798, for on 4 September, Smith reports in his diary that he was reading the "new-begun 'Stephen Calvert,' " and on the same day, Brown wrote to Dunlap that he had laid aside the story of Carwin to begin a new book, projected to be the size of *Wieland,* that he intended to complete in a month, "provided no yellow fever interpose to disconcert [his] schemes."[1] How much of *Stephen Calvert* was written at this time is not known, nor can we be sure when he again took up the work. The yellow fever did intervene, and when it was over, Brown went on to write other books. The next we hear of *Stephen Calvert* is its publication in the *Monthly Magazine,* where five installments appeared between June 1799 and January 1800. A two-month break in the publication at this point probably means that Brown had run out of manuscript and wrote the last three parts in the spring of 1800. The last installment appeared in the

June issue with the story incomplete and Brown calling the work only "the *first* act" of "a five-act drama" (6:272).[2]

What Brown intended to do with the book cannot now be determined, but it seems unlikely that he really meant to extend the story to such a length—to write a novel of a thousand pages. The book *is* incomplete, for it breaks off at a crucial scene, and a number of loose ends are left at that point. Nonetheless, the book can be read, much like the first part of *Arthur Mervyn,* as a self-contained unit that details the adventures of a young man trying to make his way in the world.[3] In this book, however, the story is told in the first person by the protagonist some time after the events have occurred. He can thus comment on the action he narrates from the point of view of an older man. Calvert has retired to the shores of Lake Michigan because he has learned from experience that the world is "too abundant in temptation and calamity for [him] safely to remain in it," that he "can escape from guilt and remorse only by interposing deserts between [himself] and the haunts of mankind" (6:71–72). He tells his story to an interested visitor who has come to his wilderness retreat.

Calvert begins his tale with an account of his family background in Europe. His overbearing and vindictive grandfather, Sir Stephen Porter, was an English Catholic who raised his older son, Henry, to be his heir and intended the younger, Stephen, to become a soldier in the service of Spain and Austria. While in Flanders, Stephen was exposed to the arguments of a Protestant minister, and he later fell in love with a French Huguenot. As a result, he renounced his religion, gave up his profession, and secretly married the woman, who bore him twin sons, Felix and Stephen. Sir Stephen, unaware of his son's apostasy, drew him into a plot to place the Stuarts again on the throne; but the son, assuming his wife's name, Calvert, fled to Pennsylvania, where, suspected by the conspirators of having betrayed the plot, he eventually met a mysterious end. In the course of the complicated process by which the family traveled to America, the twins were separated, and Felix was left with a nurse in England. The boy was abducted by old Sir Stephen, and his parents, thinking him lost to them forever, changed Stephen's name to Felix. This second Felix Calvert is the narrator of the tale.

As the story progresses, young Calvert grows up in America with his widowed mother and inherits an estate from a distant relative named Ambrose Calvert. He was a cruel man who beat his slaves, including his own black daughter, Althea, and even unjustly cast out of his house his legitimate white daughter, Louisa. Felix, an emotionally unstable boy who acts on impulse and passion, falls in love with Louisa in his imagination before he even meets her, but he abruptly changes his mind when he sees that she is short, pockmarked, and unattractive. He realizes that in justice the estate should be hers, and he even reveals at one point that he intends to give it to her, yet he cannot bring himself to part with it, and though he does not love her, he even considers proposing marriage, reconciling himself to the idea by dwelling upon her excellent character.

It is obvious that Felix is rationalizing. Like Arthur Mervyn, he is influenced in his plans for marriage by the thought of material gain. Louisa, on the other hand, does love him, and when he asks her to marry him, she immediately accepts. Their marriage is blocked by a friend, Sydney Carlton, who loves Louisa himself and who correctly points out to her that the "passionate and headstrong" Felix is as yet too unstable to be a proper partner for her. Convinced by his argument, Louisa insists that the marriage be postponed until his "character is matured by that age and experience in which [he is] now deficient" (6:137–38, 144).

Sydney is soon proved right in his judgment of Calvert's character, for Felix falls in love with Clelia Neville, whose life he has saved in a fire. Overwhelmed by Clelia's beauty and talent, which stands in sharp contrast to the homely aspect of the plain Louisa, Felix visits her often. But because he is not yet sure of the lovely Clelia, he does not cut himself off completely from his cousin, nor does he tell her of his love for Clelia. From this point on, Felix becomes increasingly ensnared in the web of deceit he has woven. When, on proposing to her, he learns that Clelia is already married, he turns to his cousin though he has not seen her for a fortnight; and, informed that Sydney and she are aware that he has been courting another woman, he tells Louisa part of the truth and assures her that he will not see Clelia again. Despite his promise, he soon begins to think of Clelia, convinces himself that there may be a reasonable explanation for her behavior, and goes to her when she sends him a letter. Swayed by whichever woman has his ear at the moment, Felix readily accepts her story that she was urged against her will into marriage with a depraved man named Belgrave and has fled to America to escape his cruelty. Felix even agrees to become her friend once more and resumes his visits.

Felix is eventually confronted with the possibility that he has been completely duped by the woman's story. For Sydney has learned, Louisa tells Felix, that Belgrave is no monster. Indeed, Clelia is said to be a profligate who retained her father's clerk as a paramour even after her marriage. When Felix goes to Sydney with the demand that he present proof of the charge, Sydney replies that he has it: Clelia is again seeing her lover in America. Felix, on his part, refuses to believe the report since he is certain that Clelia has no visitors but himself, and he and Sydney are soon at odds over the evidence which each thinks he possesses. Sydney reports that Clelia was entertaining her paramour the preceding Saturday night, and when Felix insists that it could not be true because he was with her at the time, Sydney believes that Felix is telling a deliberate lie, for *he* thinks that Felix was seen playing draughts in a tavern at the time. He does not fully reveal this piece of information, however, and Felix is dismayed when Sydney and Louisa dismiss him as a lying wretch. He is further confused when Clelia Neville, asking him questions about his past which he answers truthfully, also banishes him.

It is apparent that the other Felix has appeared on the scene and that the two are so much alike that one is easily mistaken for the other. The confusion is eventually straightened out—after a mad trip to sea, near shipwreck, and rescue on Felix's part—and the story ends just as the brothers are at the point of meeting. Brown is thus using the ancient device of unrecognized twins to ring a variation upon the theme of *Wieland:* the ease with which the senses may be deluded to lead even the best disposed persons, like Sydney Carlton,[4] to erroneous conclusions; but in *Stephen Calvert* it is sight, not hearing, which is deceived. The device, however, does not work nearly so well in this story, for certain serious difficulties obtrude. If Felix and Stephen are really so different in appearance as both Clelia and Sydney eventually recognize, one wonders how Clelia could have mistaken one for the other.[5] Indeed, if Clelia and the real Felix actually carried on an affair in Europe as they are reported to have done, it is inconceivable that she and Felix-Stephen could have established the kind of relationship described in the novel. Surely some reference to the past by Clelia would have enlightened him or at least have made him suspicious.

More important, however, than the theme of deceptive appearance is that embodied in the character of Felix Calvert: the errors of imposture and self-deception into which an impetuous youth may be led by following impulse and passion.[6] It is a theme convincingly presented through the action, but one may question whether it would have been sufficient to sustain a longer work of fiction. Felix's vacillations are interesting, but only up to a point. Transparent as he is, he lacks the complexity—and indeed the subtlety of presentation—that engages the reader's interest in Arthur Mervyn and Edgar Huntly, the heroes of Brown's books that he resembles most.[7] Granted the character and the fullness of the thematic development, it is difficult to see where the story might still have gone, for, by the end of the fragment, the point of the tale has been thoroughly made. Recent critics, to be sure, drawing on modern theories, have seen interesting possibilities in Brown's use of twins to suggest psychological doubling or to see the two

Calverts and Sydney Carlton as parts of a single personality.[8] There is, however, little evidence in the story to support such conclusions.

With the abandonment of *Stephen Calvert* and the completion of *Arthur Mervyn* in 1800, the major phase of Brown's career as a novelist was over. Many changes in both his life and his writing were soon to occur. The end of the year brought the conclusion of the third and last volume of the *Monthly Magazine,* a periodical that continued for two more years as a quarterly, renamed the *American Review and Literary Journal,* but with which Brown seems to have had no very close connection.[9] Late in 1800, Brown returned to Philadelphia to live with his brother James and to join both James and Armitt in their importing business.[10] Other changes too were in the making. Before he left New York, Brown had fallen in love with Elizabeth Linn, whom he was to marry in 1804. Indeed, even the direction of Brown's work took a new turn since the books he published in 1801 depart from the kind of work he had done in his most important fiction. Both *Clara Howard* and *Jane Talbot* are sentimental tales of love and marriage in epistolary form.

Brown was aware that the highly unusual incidents that had characterized a work like *Edgar Huntly* laid him open to criticism, for he had written his brother James in April 1800 that although James's "remarks upon the gloominess and out-of-nature incidents of Huntley [*sic*]" were perhaps "not just in their full extent," they were, "doubtless, such as most readers will make." This alone, he goes on to say, "is a sufficient reason for dropping the doleful tone and assuming a cheerful one, or, at least substituting moral causes and daily incidents in place of the prodigious or the singular. I shall not fall hereafter into that strain."[11] Though one may regret that Brown turned away from the kind of fiction in which he had achieved his greatest success, the change in his work is less dramatic than his decision implies. He had already used elements of the sentimental mode in his early books, particularly in his treatment of the heroines in *Wieland* and *Ormond,*[12] and if he was now to eschew the Gothic devices that give *Wieland* and *Edgar Huntly* their characteristic tone, he continued nonetheless the intellectual probing that lay at the thematic heart of his four major novels.

Clara Howard

Brown based his next, and shortest, book, *Clara Howard; In a Series of Letters,* on the experience one of his friends had had sometime around 1790. John Davidson, a member of the Belles Lettres Club, had become involved with two women in much the same way as Edward Hartley in the novel and turned to his friend for advice. In the account of the incident in

Paul Allen's life of Brown—a section Dunlap suppressed when he took over the biography—Brown expresses an opinion much like that maintained by Clara in the novel. In turning the incident into fiction, however, Brown altered the details in such a way as to focus attention on Clara, increase the complexity of the situation, and make her position untenable. Ten years' experience had apparently altered his views when he began to write the book, probably in New York in the late summer or fall of 1800, before his return to Philadelphia. The book was in press by late April or early May 1801, and all the evidence points to a date of publication late in June—most likely within a day or so of 22 June.[13]

The story is complicated. Edward Hartley, a poor country lad, has gained the affection of a cultivated English gentleman, Mr. E. Howard, who tutors him for a while but suddenly departs for Europe, apparently never to return. When Edward goes to the city to become a watchmaker's apprentice, he meets Mary Wilmot, a rather homely girl nine years his senior who had been reared in luxury, but who, now fallen on evil days, supports her brother and herself by sewing. Despite the difference in age, she falls in love with him, but Edward does not return her love. Nevertheless, he does consider marriage with her. Totally inexperienced with women and admiring her many good qualities, he does not realize that he may one day feel more strongly toward another. When, at her brother's death, Mary comes unexpectedly into an inheritance of five thousand dollars, Edward becomes importunate that they marry. Mary finally consents, believing that the benefit she can bestow on him with her money will compensate him for a loveless marriage. She defers the ceremony for half a year, however, so that he can be certain that he wants to go through with it.

Before that time elapses, a man named Morton appears to claim the brother's money, and Howard returns unexpectedly with a wife and beautiful stepdaughter, Clara. Now quite wealthy, Howard takes Edward into his house as his son. Mary is deeply affected by the news. Believing that her money is lost and that Edward will fare better with the young, beautiful, wealthy Clara, Mary disappears with a man named Sedley and his sister, Mrs. Valentine. She sends a letter to Edward, which is misplaced at his country home and does not come into his hands until four months later. Thus unaware of what has become of Mary, Edward considers his engagement broken and turns his attention to Clara, but when he tells her of his previous betrothal to Mary, she reacts in an unexpected manner. Full of benevolist desire to make other people happy, Clara insists that it is his duty to find Mary and to marry her if her happiness demands it. She is convinced that she can never be happy herself if her joy must be bought by

Mary's unhappiness. Therefore, although she too loves Edward, she refuses to marry him while Mary is single and unhappy. She even demands that he persuade Mary to marry him and offers them half her fortune so that she—Clara—can enjoy the pleasure of sacrificing herself to another's happiness (5:7, 24, 71–72).

Edward is thus presented with an absurd situation: forced by the woman he loves to find and perhaps marry one he does not love and who has disappeared without a trace. But he does what Clara demands and eventually finds Mary's misplaced letter. So full is it of heartbreak and threats of dying because of the calamity which has befallen her that Edward resolves at first to go through with the proposal. Thoughts of Clara deter him, and he finally decides to find Mary and restore the money, which, he has recently learned, Morton will not claim. Before he can perform this duty, Edward falls sick with a fever, contracted while saving a girl from drowning, and lies near death. Clara, horrified at the thought that he might die, relents in the demands she has made and summons him back to her, though not without some fears that she is doing an injustice to Mary. Edward is overjoyed at the news but wants first to find Mary and restore her funds to her. Clara, however, runs into Mary at the house of an acquaintance. Without even asking her condition, she assumes that she is still single and unhappy, and she demands once again that Edward persuade her to marry him.

What neither Edward nor Clara knows is that Mary's condition has changed. She has learned from Mrs. Valentine, with whom she has been staying, that the five thousand dollars is really hers, the gift of Sedley, who has long loved Mary and who had used the roundabout means of helping her by sending the sum anonymously to her brother. Impressed by his generosity—he knew that the money might be used to support her and Edward—Mary begins at last to feel affection for him. Convinced by Mrs. Valentine, whose name is surely significant, of the folly of longing for one who does not return her affection, she finally agrees to marry Sedley. Before Edward learns of Mary's decision, he rushes to propose to her, for he has become convinced that Clara cannot love him and act the way she does. He goes through a period of torment when it looks as if neither woman will have him: Clara, because she thinks Mary is unhappy; Mary, because she has renounced him to Clara. Caught in the middle and hurrying away from Mary before she has a chance to explain her new plans, Edward resolves, like Stephen Calvert, to disappear into the wilderness. But before he has hardly started, he falls ill on the way, and letters catch up with him to reveal the truth: that Mary will marry Sedley and be happy. The impediment thus removed, Clara welcomes him with open arms, and the book ends with plans being made for two weddings.

It is difficult to take such a story seriously today. The overwrought emotionalism of the characters is not to the modern taste, and their vacillations seem absurd. Brown also made the mistake of including in *Clara Howard* material that he had already used in *Edgar Huntly.* Edward Hartley, like the protagonist of the earlier book, lives with an uncle who supports him and his sisters but whose son has developed such an implacable enmity toward them that they will be cast off the farm when his father dies (5:47). In a similar fashion, Edward and Mary, like Huntly and Mary Waldegrave, depend for their future on a mysterious sum of money left by the girl's dead brother. Wilmot, like Waldegrave, courts poverty while doing good to others, and Morton, like Weymouth, consigns a sum of money to his friend before being shipwrecked on the other side of the Atlantic. Details differ, of course, in the two incidents, and the claim in the later book turns out to be false. But Brown's use of the material a second time can hardly be said to strengthen *Clara Howard* as a work of fiction.

Yet *Clara Howard* should not be dismissed without further attention, for the novel is not without interest. In this book, as in *Arthur Mervyn,* there is a strange contradiction between the characters' acts and their professions of principle. Clara Howard insists that reason alone must guide their actions, that rationality demands both the sacrifice of her happiness to Mary's and Edward's willing performance of the duty she lays upon him, but the action of the book indicates that she is no more immune to emotionalism than the others. One wonders, for example, whether the ultimate reason for the demands she makes on Edward does not derive in part from an emotional identification with Mary's plight, since she believes it is her duty "to judge of the feelings of others by her own" (5:71). Clara knows, moreover, the pleasures of both wealth and love, so that she can imagine—she tells Edward at one point—what it would be like to lose both, as Mary has (5:77). Her sympathy for what she thinks are Mary's sufferings seems to be at least one important influence in motivating her to act as she does.

Nor is this the only incident in which Clara gives way to her emotions. When she first sends Edward off to seek the unfortunate Mary, she is adamant in demanding that he do what she prescribes. He must "zealously solicit" a union with Mary or else be unworthy of her love and esteem, and he must not imagine that any appeal to her sympathy or pity will lead her to change her mind (5:20–21). But when Edward falls seriously ill and almost dies, Clara forgets all her firm resolutions and begs him to come to her: "The arms of thy Clara are open to receive thee. She is ready to kneel to thee for pardon; to expiate her former obduracy by tears of gratitude and tenderness. Lay on my past offences what penalty thou wilt. The heavier it be the more cheerfully shall I sustain it; the more adequate it will be to my fault" (5:34). Clara's new resolutions last only a little while. No sooner does she meet Mary than she assumes without asking that Mary is still unhappy, and, apparently as the result of her emotional reaction on seeing the girl, she makes her absurd demands on Edward a second time. None of these actions is the result of rational choice.

In the light of such evidence, we cannot assume that Clara Howard is a force of reason or of rational duty in the novel—nor can we conclude with David Lee Clark that she is "Brown's ideal woman," or a "humanized Constantia Dudley."[14] A better interpretation of Clara's behavior is that suggested by Sydney J. Krause, who sees her as a proponent of the philosophy of William Godwin, especially as it was expressed in *Political Justice*. If Krause's reading of Clara is correct, Brown is returning in this book to the Godwinian philosophy that influenced him so strongly when he began his career as a novelist. In *Clara Howard,* however, he is no longer professing his belief in it. He puts it instead to the test of consequences and finds it wanting. Clara is determined to practice the Godwinian theory of disinterested benevolence in her relations with others, but her attempt succeeds only in creating a moral conflict and involving the characters in contradictions from which they cannot escape. Yet Clara does not learn from her experience. She remains the thoroughgoing Godwinian right to the end, even though her intellectual position has been completely demolished.[15]

Though Krause's interpretation is cogently argued, readers today do not need a knowledge of Godwin to understand the book. The objections to Clara's position are voiced in the novel through a letter Edward writes to her after she makes her demands on him a second time. Though Mary and Clara both call him rash and impetuous—judgments justified by some of his actions—in this carefully reasoned letter Edward talks sense to Clara, and he emerges as a believable character to the extent that he does so. He points out to her that she is wrong in the decision she has made. Though her motives may be pure, her "judgment . . . is misguided." It is absurd, he argues, for her to believe that she can secure Mary's happiness by urging him to marry her. Even if Mary should consent to the union (an unlikely event), only unhappiness would come to her from an unloving husband. Besides, Edward goes on to say, Clara acts as if Mary alone is worthy of benevolent treatment—that only Mary's wishes and not his are to be considered (5:110–12).

After all, Edward continues, he has the same claim on Clara's affections as Mary has on his, so that if he is "cruel and unjust, in refusing [his] love to one that claims it," then so is Clara in refusing to give her love to him, because "the rule is fallacious that is not applicable to all others in the same circumstances." In addition, Mary and he are not the only ones affected by her decision; Sedley has precisely the same claim on Mary's affections as Mary has on Edward's. "For him and for me, your benevolence sleeps. With regard to us you have neither consideration nor humanity. They are all absorbed in the cause of one, whose merits, whose claim to your sympathy and aid, if it be not less, is far from being greater than Sedley's or mine" (5:112–13). Thus, Edward makes clear to Clara that he thinks her completely wrong in her estimate of where her duty lies.

Yet Edward's very rationality in this letter causes a problem in interpretation, for if his estimate of Clara's error is as just as it seems, why does he submit to what he calls her better judgment at the end of the book? When Clara summons him back to her in the closing pages, she soundly berates him for planning to go West, and she argues that he must return to her and make her forget his errors "by the rectitude of [his] future conduct" (5:141). Edward replies that he will hurry to her at once and asks her forgiveness. At this point we may assume that Edward is motivated by his love for her, but when he accepts without a murmur the assumption of leadership on the part of one whose judgment in an important matter he has already shown to be in error, one wonders what possesses him. Clara is determined to lead in the marriage. "My maturer age and more cautious judgment," she writes to him, "shall be counsellers and guides to thy inexperienced youth. While I love thee and cherish thee as a wife, I shall assume some of the prerogatives of an elder sister, and put my circumspection and forethought in the balance against thy headlong confidence." She believes that his genius and knowledge will enable him to surpass her in the not very distant future, but for the time being at least, she claims "to be more than equal" to him "in moral discernment." The implication is strong that she expects him to conform to her views (5:147).

Why Edward will accept her under these circumstances is not easy to understand, but accept her he does without a demur—a decision that needs explanation. The conflict between his actions here and his earlier estimate of her erroneous judgment must somehow be reconciled unless one wishes to dismiss his conduct as utterly inconsistent or hopelessly confused by romantic love. There is some evidence to suggest, however, that Edward Hartley knows what he is about, that, like Arthur Mervyn or, indeed, Stephen Calvert when he first wooed Louisa, he is at least as much interested in money as he is in a wife. He first becomes determined to wed Mary when she inherits the five thousand dollars from her brother, only to turn his attention to the more beautiful—and rich—Clara when she appears. Indeed, in one of his letters to Clara, he mentions her wealth, disavows any wish to control it, and sees it as his glory and boast to submit to one he considers "unerring and divine. Clara's will is my law" (5:89–90). Even before his final submission to her, he has already linked her wealth with a determination to do as she wishes.

The book's introduction points in the same direction, for in it Edward writes to a friend to tell him of his good fortune at having acquired a wealthy wife and sends the packet of letters that make up the book. Just three years before, Edward was only "a simple lad" who worked as a watchmaker. Without friends or property, he was "full of that rustic diffidence, that inveterate humility, which are alone sufficient to divert from us the stream of fortune's favours." But everything has changed: "Now I am rich, happy, crowned with every terrestrial felicity, in possession of that most exquisite of all blessings, a wife, endowed with youth, grace, dignity, discretion." He accepts his good fortune, moreover, with a disavowal of any merit on his own part. "It was impossible for me to have foreseen, absurd to have hoped for such a destiny. All that has happened, was equally beyond my expectations and deservings" (5:3). This statement has something of the sound of Arthur Mervyn, who managed to place himself in a similar position of wealth. It suggests that Edward Hartley too may have more than a bit of the opportunist in his makeup.

Such an interpretation demands that a strain of irony be seen as running through the book, and one must be cautious in seeing Brown as a conscious ironist. Nonetheless, the alternative is to read *Clara Howard* as a rather poor piece of sentimental fiction with an absurd plot designed merely to illustrate, in an echo of *Stephen Calvert,* the "enthusiasm"—in the eighteenth-century sense—of those in love.[16] Certainly, much of the action of the book can be explained in these terms, and the characters of Edward Hartley and, more especially, Clara Howard bear some resemblance to that of the emotionally volatile Calvert. Yet there is, without question, more to the book than that. Nothing that Brown wrote was without intellectual interest, and although modern readers may not find the conventions of sentimental fiction attractive, Brown's use of them in *Clara Howard* may have been the appropriate means for testing the theory of disinterested benevolence that Clara attempts to practice. The failure of her efforts and the success of Edward Hartley, who, like Arthur Mervyn, acts in his own self-interest, show unmistakably the conclusions Brown had reached on the validity of Godwinian philosophy.

Jane Talbot

It is not entirely clear when Brown wrote *Jane Talbot,* his last novel. Since, in a letter to Elizabeth Linn of 10 March 1801, he mentions his decision not to publish the book, a change of plans he would explain to her later, we must assume that it was at least begun before that date, but we do not know when or how much of the book he might already have written. He seems to have laid the novel aside while he worked on *Clara Howard,* for in late June, just around the time that *Clara Howard* was published, we learn from the *Travels* of John Davis, an Englishman who visited him in Philadelphia, that Brown was then at work on a novel that Davis does not name but almost certainly was *Jane Talbot.* Nothing more is heard of the book until 21 August, when it was announced as "in the press," but Brown may well have continued to work on it into the fall because it was not advertised for sale until mid-December. We can conclude from these facts that Brown worked on *Jane Talbot, a Novel* throughout 1801 and published it in December of that year.[17]

Jane Talbot resembles *Clara Howard* in its sentimental subject matter and method of presentation. The central concern of the plot is the same problem of sentimental fiction—proper marriage for the heroine—and both stories are told through the epistolary technique. As in *Clara Howard,* too, Brown uses the book to examine the Godwinian philosophy that had so attracted him in the 1790s, and Krause has shown that in this novel, as in the previous one, Brown tests the philosophy and records its failure.[18] Yet despite these similarities, *Jane Talbot* is today a much more interesting book. The problem of intellectual and religious incompatibility that Henry Colden and Jane Talbot confront seems a great deal more serious than any faced by Edward Hartley and Clara Howard; the objections to Colden raised by Mrs. Fielder, Jane's adopted mother, create a complication more understandable than any introduced in the earlier book; and the actions of Colden and Jane are considerably more believable than those of Edward and Clara. Though *Jane Talbot* may seem to be as dated as *Clara Howard,* it is developed in terms that are far more acceptable to modern readers.

The plot is simple. Jane Talbot, a young widow, is in love with Henry Colden, but their marriage is opposed first by Mrs. Fielder, who has reared her since childhood, and later by Colden's father. The grounds for objection are serious. Mrs. Fielder has seen some letters that Colden had written to a friend named Thomson which reveal that he has been arguing vigorously in favor of the radical doctrine expounded in Godwin's *Political Justice.* He has shown himself to be, in Mrs. Fielder's words, "the advocate of suicide; a scoffer at promises; the despiser of revelation, of providence and a future state; an opponent of marriage"; and a defender of sexual enormities. He even feels it incumbent upon him as a duty "to preach, with vehemence, his new faith." Indeed, so strong had his belief in the new ideas become that "the rage for making converts seized him, and that Thomson was not won over to the same cause, proceeded from no want of industry in Colden" (5:227–28). The hero of the book, therefore, would seem to be a radical thinker of the school we are already familiar with, in general, from its appearance in other works by Brown.[19]

Mrs. Fielder has reason to believe that Jane has already been strongly influenced by Colden's radical views, and she has seen evidence to convince her that Colden has even induced Jane to put them into practice. Lewis Talbot, Jane's husband, had, before his death, shown Mrs. Fielder a letter Jane had supposedly written to Colden that would clearly indicate—were not part of it a forgery—that Jane and Colden had fallen into adultery. It seems that one night while Talbot was away on business, Colden had visited Jane, and, a severe storm arising, he had been allowed to spend the night under her roof. The following day Jane had begun a letter to Colden, mentioning the fact that he had stayed the night. But the letter was stolen before she had had a chance to finish it, and the thief forged a conclusion that can only be construed as proving their supposed guilt. Because Colden is known to have radical views, Mrs. Fielder lends credence to the letter, believes in Jane's fall, and urges her not to marry her "seducer" lest he drag her further down to sin and shame.

Most of the story, as one would expect, is concerned with the revelation of these events through the letters the characters write. Mrs. Fielder, in New York, urges Jane, who lives in Philadelphia, to return to her. Meanwhile, Colden, who is visiting the dying Thomson in Wilmington, writes to Jane, urging his love and sincerity. He eventually reveals that he no longer holds the views attributed to him. Jane, torn between love and duty, vacillates between the two, and the story in effect stands still while the characters discuss their problem in long letters. Eventually the problems are all resolved in favor of the lovers. Colden discovers that the forger is a Miss Jessup, who loved Talbot and sought to estrange him from his wife. She confesses the deed in a letter to Colden, which she later denies as a forgery, and Mrs. Fielder, who accepts her assertion that Colden forged the confession, considers his supposed act as yet another proof of his depravity. Jane and Colden are separated soon thereafter, when he goes to sea. While he is gone, Miss Jessup makes a deathbed confession, and Mrs. Fielder, learning the truth of her daughter's innocence, asks forgiveness for having doubted her. When Colden finally returns, he and Jane are free to marry.

Described thus baldly, the novel would seem to be a conventional sentimental tale, completely different from the original work that Brown had done in his four major books. *Jane Talbot,* however, has something more to offer modern readers than the marriage problem of Jane and Colden, which is of only secondary interest in the book. More important are the questions Brown raises on the strengths and limitations of reason and emotion as guides to life and the discussion he includes on the value of religious faith as the foundation for proper behavior. These issues had been important in Brown's earlier fiction, for he had questioned radical rationalist views in a number of his books, and in *Ormond* he had even suggested the need for a religious view of life to counter such opinions. Now at last, at the end of his brief career as a novelist, he answers the questions he had previously raised and brings both his intellectual quest and his career to a close.[20]

Brown is doing more in *Jane Talbot* than writing a love story. Jane Talbot and Henry Colden have intellectual as well as romantic roles to play in the novel, and their final union represents the resolution of a real philosophic question. Colden represents the rationalist view, which, once it has infected the individual, leads him away from religious faith and turns him into a skeptic. Colden has indeed, as Mrs. Fielder believes, fallen under the influence of Godwin's thought. Experience, however, has made him question the validity of Godwin's views, but he still remains something of a rationalist who cannot accept, though he does not oppose, religious faith. Jane considers his "propensity to reason" as one of his faults (5:309) and would like him to show more signs of emotion. She believes he needs "a little more impetuosity and fervour" in his love. He is "not quite passionate enough," she tells him. "Love has not banished discretion, or blindfolded your sagacity" (5:208). Even in loving Jane, he maintains control of his reason, and, in general, he provides a balance to the more volatile Jane.

She is precisely the opposite. "I am very far from being a wise girl," she writes in the first line of the novel, and much of what ensues supports her opinion. Indeed, the first incidents she relates, her early life with her father and brother, serve only to confirm it. After her mother's death and her adoption by Mrs. Fielder, Jane's father retired from business, and Jane was horrified to see her brother, Frank, unrestrained by a weak and overly lenient father, spend his own money foolishly, embezzle and waste sums intended for a cousin, and wheedle from his parent not only the income from his investments but even the capital itself. It is apparent to all—and not least to Jane—that Frank, hopelessly corrupted by riotous living, is insatiable in his desire for money. When, all other sources having been exhausted, he approaches Jane herself and asks for the loan of five hundred dollars from a legacy she possesses, she is well aware what her answer should be—"I harboured not a moment's doubt as to the conduct it became me to pursue" (5:179)—and, when he persists with his importunities, she asserts her determination not to part with her money (5:181).

Despite her knowledge of her brother's character and her good resolutions, Jane eventually relents when he appeals repeatedly to her emotions, for her heart, she writes, "is the sport, the mere plaything of gratitude and pity. Kindness will melt my firmest resolutions in a moment" (5:182). Although Jane does not give in at the first appeal to her sympathy, she is incapable of resisting his pleas for long. Eventually she begins to think that she is being too cautious, that her brother really does need her help, and, when he finally looks at her with deep distress in his face, she begs his forgiveness and gives him the money he asks—only to regret the act immediately. Such emotionalism and irresolution are basic to Jane's character, and despite the fact that she learns the sum was wasted, she lends him money twice more—and almost succumbs a fourth time before her mother takes matters into her own hands and drives Frank away. Mrs. Fielder has thus had ample opportunity to observe the "impetuosity of feeling which distinguished [Jane's] early age" (5:226), a sensibility that, she believed, required "strict government" (5:223).

Convinced that Jane must be protected against her own temperament, Mrs. Fielder urged her into a loveless marriage with a somewhat stolid man almost twice her age. That Jane was not cured of her emotionalism by this marriage is testified to by her strong attraction to Colden after her husband's death and by her inability to resist the opposite emotional pulls of either Colden or Mrs. Fielder. Even as a grown woman and widow, Jane is unable to form a resolution and stick to it in the face of appeals to feelings. At the urging of Mrs. Fielder, she vows "an eternal separation from Colden" (5:239), yet a word from him destroys her determination. "No will, no reason have I of my own," she writes (5:256), a judgment confirmed by Colden himself, who, when she renounces him a second time, observes to his brother-in-law: "There are but two persons in the world who command her affections. Either when present, (the other absent or silent) has absolute dominion over her" (5:326). Rather than continue the struggle for Jane's allegiance, Colden accepts his dismissal, embarks upon a long voyage to the Pacific, and leaves Jane completely under the dominance of Mrs. Fielder.

But although Jane Talbot is—like Stephen Calvert and, to a certain extent, Clara Howard—primarily a creature of emotion throughout most of the novel, she is indirectly influenced to more rational views by her experience with Henry Colden. Jane has apparently always been a deeply religious person, and she had even objected at first to marrying Talbot because, although he was a good man in his personal conduct, he lacked ardor and conviction in his religious belief and practice. Jane possesses the fervor that was wanting in her husband, but until she meets Colden, she does not seem to have considered the rational grounds for her belief. When she attempts to lead Colden back to faith, she is shocked to discover that she has no foundation for her principles. Once aware of this fact, she "instantly set [herself] to the business of enquiry," for she suddenly realized that she could not influence his convictions if she did not know the basis for her own. She was aware that she ran a risk in arguing with an unbeliever intellectually stronger than she, but she did not fall prey to his delusions. Rather, she thinks, her "belief is stronger than it ever was" because of her experience (5:306–8).

While Jane is finding a rational basis for her piety, she also learns an important lesson about human beings. Before she had met Colden, she had followed Mrs. Fielder in considering every unbeliever a black-hearted wretch to be scorned and avoided. She had not thought it possible to love such a person, yet she quickly learns that although she may still "regard unbelief as the blackest stain; as the most deplorable calamity that can befall a human creature," she may nonetheless still love the man as a human being. Her love brings with it the obligation "to rescue him from this calamity" (5:302–3). Jane, in a sense, is humanized by this perception in a way that Mrs. Fielder is not until the end of her life when she asks forgiveness. For Jane ceases to "hold in scorn or abhorrence those who differ from [her]." Instead, she writes: "I find it possible for men to disbelieve and yet retain their claims to our reverence, our affection, and especially our good offices" (5:307). In short, though she still condemns his error, she does not hate or revile the man who commits it, for he still has a claim to her respect for his humanity.[21]

Just as Jane is brought to more humane and more rational views as a result of her acquaintance with Colden, so also is he led toward faith by Jane and the others he associates with in the story. The change, however, is not sudden, nor is it initiated by them. He had already moved away from his radical opinions by the time the action of the novel begins, so that Jane's influence only confirms a step he has himself taken. As Jane writes to him at one point, his "own experience had half converted [him] already"; and a closer look at the theories that had ensnared him showed "flaws and discords" that led him to abandon the radical extreme (5:306–7). Thus, "you err," she observes, "but are not obstinate in error. If your opinions be adverse to religion, your affections are not wholly estranged from it. Your understanding dissents, but your heart is not yet persuaded to refuse" (5:304). At this stage of his intellectual development, he is ready to listen to Jane with "unprejudiced attention"—indeed, even with a bias in favor of her opinions (5:306), and, although it is by no means Jane alone who converts him, she is certainly instrumental in helping him when others, like Mrs. Fielder, would have cast him aside without a hearing.

Of great, if not equal, importance is the influence of Colden's friend Thomson, whom he had once tried to convert to disbelief. Colden is in Wilmington at his dying friend's side when we first meet him, for Thomson had summoned him "to urge . . . the truths of religion, at a time when his own conduct might visibly attest their value." Though Thomson suffers much, Colden notes that "his closing hour is serene. His piety now stands him in some stead." Colden insists that he is not so much the enemy of Thomson's views as his friend seems to think (5:275–76), and as he later writes, he listens attentively to Thomson's "arguments and admonitions . . . with a suitable spirit." Colden does not think him wrong. Indeed, he goes on to say, "at any time I should have allowed infinite plausibility and subtilty to his reasonings, and at this time, I confessed them to be weighty." Because he is deeply concerned about his friend's death and about the uncertainty of his relation to Jane, he makes no immediate decision as to their truth but treasures them for future thought (5:387).

His opportunity for thinking comes when he goes on his long journey to the Pacific, a voyage he embarks upon because his doubts remain. Thomson's sister, Harriet, advises him to stay away from Jane because Mrs. Fielder's objections to him are not "without just grounds." As Harriet points out to him, any change in his views "must necessarily be slow and gradual," and time might eventually remove the obstacles that stand in the way of their marriage (5:391–92). Colden is gone longer than he expects, however. Because of a mutiny on board the vessel, he is put ashore on a desert island and is eventually taken to Japan by some fishermen. Before he can make his way home again by way of Batavia and Hamburg, four years have elapsed and a radical change has taken place in his intellectual development. "The incidents of a long voyage," he writes to his brother-in-law on his return, "the vicissitudes through which I have passed have given strength to my frame, while the opportunities and occasions for wisdom which these have afforded me, have made *my mind whole*. I have awakened from my dreams of doubt and misery, not to the cold and vague belief, but to the living and delightful consciousness of every tie that can bind man to his divine parent and judge" (5:427).

Although Colden does not detail the steps through which he has gone in achieving his newly won faith, he does make clear to his brother-in-law that this change is permanent. He hopes by his conduct to be as good an example to others as some have been to him, and he believes that "indefatigable zeal and strenuous efforts are indeed incumbent on [him] in proportion to the extent of [his] past misconduct, and the depth of [his] former degeneracy" (5:428). His return to faith has brought him close to Jane in fundamental belief so that their long-delayed marriage can now take place. When it occurs, the union of Jane and Colden will represent the meeting on a kind of middle ground of the two approaches to life they have represented in the book, for just as Jane's experience saves her from the extremes of emotionalism and vacillation, so also does Colden's retrieve him from the rationalism of his former life. Head and heart—in an anticipation of Hawthorne and Melville[22]—will thus be united when Jane and Colden wed.

It is not only Hawthorne and Melville whose works are foreshadowed in this book, since *Jane Talbot* bears an even stronger relation to two of Cooper's novels. Henry Colden's return to faith as the result of a distant voyage looks forward to Roswell Gardiner's similar experience in Cooper's *The Sea Lions,* and the problem of lovers divided by a difference in religious belief appears as well in *The Wing-and-Wing.* Unlike Cooper, Brown does not mark out the steps in Colden's religious development, nor does he detail in any concrete way the nature of his belief. With Cooper, the issue involved was always entirely clear. In *The Wing-and-Wing,* the separated lovers are atheist and Roman Catholic and remain inevitably apart; in *The Sea Lions,* Gardiner returns to the Trinitarian faith of his sweetheart after having denied the divinity of Christ. Brown is not so specific in his development of the theme, and one can level the charge against his conclusion that the religious faith affirmed is so vague as to obscure, to some extent, the conflict between the lovers, which in Cooper's works was always precisely defined.

Yet despite the importance of *Jane Talbot* both in the development of Brown's thought and in foreshadowing some important themes in subsequent writers, the novel, like *Clara Howard,* continues to present problems for Brown's critics. Both books depart so markedly from the kind of fiction that Brown had previously written that commentators on his fiction have long treated them as inferior to his major works.[23] Some recent critics, however, have found much to praise in the books. Robert E. Hemenway and Joseph Katz see in them an affirmation of moral and social order that is in strong contrast to the "chaos and uncertainty" found in the Gothic romances.[24] Drawing a similar conclusion on the books' social and moral themes, Paul Witherington believes that the novels are the logical culmination of

Brown's career as a writer of fiction, and he goes so far as to assert that their "excellence of structure, point of view, and characterization" make them Brown's "most mature novels."[25] And Sydney J. Krause, as we have seen, has argued persuasively that the books are, when rightly understood, skillful analyses of the failure of Godwinian philosophy to meet the test of consequences.

All of these critical views have their interest, for they tell us much about the intellectual milieu out of which the novels arose and their place in the development of Brown's career. But the test of a book is in the reading, and for readers today the sentimental form and tone will continue to prove a stumbling block to a full appreciation of the novels. One can argue, of course, that the epistolary form is appropriate to books in which different ideas are proposed and contested, but it is also true that it poses problems, especially when long passages of retrospective narrative must be reported and when the various correspondents must be kept apart by fortuitous illness or accident. Though the novels are tight in structure, they are weak in action, and *Jane Talbot,* in particular, though undoubtedly the better book, is essentially static. In ruling out of his art such extraordinary elements as ventriloquism or sleepwalking and such effective real events as the yellow fever or Indian warfare, Brown abandoned the very devices that have made his first four novels attractive to the modern reader. Viewed in relation to them, *Clara Howard* and *Jane Talbot* must always seem inferior.

Chapter Seven
Coda

In concentrating our attention on the major fiction of Charles Brockden Brown, we have passed over in silence a number of his minor works, many of which were undoubtedly written while his novels were appearing. Much of this writing was published in the *Monthly Magazine,*[1] of which Brown was editor, but some was not printed until it appeared in Dunlap's *Life* in 1815,[2] and one piece in particular, "Death of Cicero: A Fragment," was even used as a filler in an early edition of *Edgar Huntly.*[3] Though all of these short works contribute something to an understanding of Brown and to an appreciation of his literary talent, only a few are of much interest today. "Thessalonica: A Roman Story" is worthy of note because of its theme: the disastrous results that can come from a minor cause because of the passions of men; and "A Lesson on Concealment; or, Memoirs of Mary Selwyn" is of special importance because, as Berthoff has shown, it illustrates so clearly the complexity of Brown's themes and the nature of his fictional method.[4] "A Lesson on Concealment" is probably the best of the group, but even it is of relatively slight importance when seen in relation to the novels which mark Brown's major achievement.

Final Works

The same judgment can also be made on the kind of writing Brown did after the appearance of *Jane Talbot.* Most interesting is a group of quasi-historical fragments that may have been started earlier, but a major portion of which, Berthoff conjectures, was very likely written between 1803 and 1807.[5] These pieces, most of which were printed in Dunlap as "Sketches of a History of Carsol" and "Sketches of a History of the Carrils and Ormes,"[6] are strange accounts of imaginary history, but Brown treats them throughout as if he were reporting facts. The time sequence is not properly maintained, and episodes follow one another with little explicit connection between them—almost as if the sketches were a group of fragments that happen to have been printed in this order.[7] They reveal a strong concern with political and religious matters, much more so than do any of Brown's novels, but though the tenor of the pieces is generally conservative, Brown takes no stand for or against any of the systems presented. He maintains, rather, the mask of objective chronicler throughout. As an odd kind of imaginary history, which may indicate, as Berthoff suggests, the direction of Brown's thinking in his later years,[8] the works are not without interest. The confused state of the fragments, on the other hand, precludes their being given the careful attention accorded Brown's major fiction.

The other writing that Brown did in the last years of his life was largely nonliterary.[9] Between 1803 and 1809 he issued a number of political pamphlets on important concerns of the day. In 1804 he published a translation of the comte de Volney's *A View of the Soil and Climate of the United States,* in which, through the use of numerous footnotes and the alteration of an appendix, he refuted some of Volney's contentions about America and advanced his own nationalistic views on the territorial expansion of the United States and its destiny as a nation.[10] And in 1805 he published the "Sketch of the Life and Character of John Blair Linn"—his wife's brother, who had died the previous year—as an introduction to an edition of Linn's poem *Valerian.*

The pamphlets are especially important for what they reveal about Brown's political interests. The first, published in January 1803, reveals American concern over the prospect of French control of Louisiana. Word had got out that by a secret treaty, Spain had ceded the territory to France. The danger the United States faced once France should take possession was brought home to Americans when, in October 1802, a Spanish official at New Orleans withdrew the right of deposit American traders had enjoyed at that port. Since western Americans relied on the Mississippi River to export their goods, such a powerful nation as France could choke off that trade at will and would always pose a threat to the western states. In *An Address to the Government of the United States on the Cession of Louisiana to the French,* Brown stressed the imminent peril by using a literary device. Assuming the persona of a French counselor of state, Brown wrote what purported to be a document addressed to Napolean on the value of Louisiana and the advantages that could accrue to France from its possession. With his point thus made, Brown had only to conclude by speaking out as an American to urge that the United States act to remove the impending threat.

In the pamphlet that quickly followed in March—*Monroe's Embassy; or, The Conduct of the Government in Relation to Our Claims to the Navigation of the Missisippi*—Brown argues even more hotly for open war. Rather than send an emissary to Europe to negotiate the issue or to buy the territory, he writes, the United States should seize Louisiana at once and defend it against the French. Both of the pamphlets on Louisiana are effective political pieces that reveal a Brown quite different from the one who wrote the novels. Even the calmer pamphlets that Brown wrote several years later show a side of the novelist that should not be forgotten. *The British Treaty* (1807), which argues the superiority of the Jay Treaty of 1794 to that negotiated with Great Britain in 1806,[11] and *An Address to the Congress of the United States on the Utility and Justice of Restrictions upon Foreign Commerce* (1809), which takes a stand against the Embargo Act of 1807, are written in a kind of straightforward style seldom, if ever, apparent in his fiction. They certainly illustrate that Brown was quite at home in political controversy.

Much of Brown's work in these later years was editorial. In October 1803 he began to publish the second of his journals, the *Literary Magazine and American Register,* which he continued to edit until 1807, when he abandoned the magazine in favor of *The American Register, or General Repository of History, Politics, and Science.* Five semiannual volumes of this work appeared between November 1807 and his death early in 1810. Both show Brown's shift of interest away from the purely literary; except for the *Memoirs of Carwin,* which appeared, somewhat irregularly, in the former between November 1803 and March 1805, Brown published little original fiction in the *Literary Magazine.*[12] By the time he took up *The American Register,* he had become absorbed in writing historical annals, and he published in this journal historical surveys of the periods covered by the volumes, digests of laws, and reports of books published both here and abroad. Indeed, at the time of his death, he had completed a large amount of work on yet another project, *A System of General Geography,* which further illustrates his turning away from the writing of fiction.[13]

Brown's last years were thus spent mostly in historical writing and editing, and although this work should certainly not be dismissed as insignificant, it does represent a falling off from the truly important fiction he had already written. Yet Brown was probably not unhappy with the change. In the first issue of the *Literary Magazine* in 1803, he made the astonishing statement that he would have more respect for himself if nothing he had written could be traced to him, and he included the enigmatic comment that he took "much blame" to himself for something he had written.[14] Brown apparently did not regret abandoning fiction.

Despite his increasing illness, too, he seems to have been relatively happy. His marriage to Elizabeth Linn in 1804 and the birth of his four children—including twin sons and a daughter—brought him comfort and happiness. His health, however, always poor, began to fail, and although he made several journeys in an attempt to regain it, he did not succeed. In November 1809, he took to his bed and lingered for several months. He showed increasing signs of advanced tuberculosis and died, fully conscious until the end, on 21 February 1810,[15] at the age of thirty-nine.

A General Assessment

The life of Charles Brockden Brown was thus short but unusually productive. Even if one dismisses most of his minor fiction and editorial work as of relatively little significance to the general student today, his six completed novels and *Stephen Calvert* are still worthy of critical attention. Brown is not by any means a major writer, and readers of his fiction must be willing to accept serious faults in plotting, style, and characterization that they would not tolerate in more recent authors. Brown's books are admittedly defective, but considering the time and the conditions under which they were written, they represent a truly important accomplishment. Not that Brown's books must be valued because they are old or because they represent the first significant achievement of an American novelist. Although such considerations undoubtedly play a part in any defense one might choose to make of his fiction, Brown's major novels deserve to be read not only for the interest they generate in their thematic development but also for the literary value which they certainly possess.

Any sound estimate of Brown's achievement must start with his themes, for his books are novels of ideas that impress one most strongly at first for the intellectuality they clearly exhibit. This quality goes far beyond the simple exposition of radical doctrine that Clark sees in the books or even the aphoristic power that Warfel observes in them.[16] Brown's examination of ideas in his fiction is much more fundamental than either of these views reveals; for, as Berthoff has correctly observed, the novels were themselves the testing grounds of ideas: vehicles not for the exposition but for the scrutiny of them.[17] If one reads the books in these terms, one soon observes that Brown's treatment of contemporary ideas tends to proceed as if he were examining the relative strengths and weaknesses of opposite points of view. His characters, thus, are spread across the whole intellectual spectrum: they frequently represent one or another extreme of human behavior. One sees in them the influence of the rational and nonrational in human experience, of mind and feeling, of belief and unbelief, of benevolence and selfishness. All of his books, it seems fair to say, represent Brown's attempt to determine for himself the significance of each element in human behavior.

The most important question he raises, in view of his background and bent of mind, is the value of reason as a guide to life. That Brown firmly believed in the validity of human reason cannot be doubted, for even in books like *Wieland* and *Edgar Huntly,* which seem almost to represent the triumph of unreason, rationality is firmly in control once again at the end of the book. Many of the characters he presents as most attractive—like Clara Wieland or Constantia Dudley—are fundamentally rationalistic in their thinking, and, with the latter heroine, Brown clearly indicates his belief that a rational education for a young woman is absolutely necessary if she is to survive in the practical world. Departures from reason are always considered abnormalities in Brown's fiction, and his last novel, *Jane Talbot,* which may justly be taken to reflect his final intellectual position, clearly indicates his belief in the need for a rational basis for faith to protect the human being from the extremes of emotionalism. The point need not be dwelled upon. The whole direction of Brown's intellectual life and the development of his thought as it is revealed throughout his fiction clearly indicate the central position he would grant to human reason as a primary element in leading human beings to truth and guiding their actions.

This is not to say that Brown was, or remained for long, a naive rationalist, for the evidence is conclusive that he saw some serious dangers in the paths of those who would attempt to lead the utterly rational life—a point underscored in a number of his books. Even his strongest rationalists sometimes get into trouble when they try to draw conclusions on the basis of sensory evidence with their minds alone. The influence of early impressions affects such characters as Clara and Theodore Wieland; the usual human passions lead Henry Pleyel astray. Even Constantia Dudley, who is obviously intended to represent the best and most rational of them all, nearly fails in the most important crisis of her life because, for all her rationality, she cannot hope to meet and overcome with her mind alone the insidious attacks on her virtue launched by the deceitful Ormond. All of these characters have strong intellects, and all have been given what is supposed to be a superior education—yet all fail in meeting the challenge presented to their minds by what they see and hear in the external world. Their failure, then, one may conclude, clearly represents Brown's serious doubts that weak and fallible human beings can always arrive at truth simply through the use of their unaided minds.

An even more serious indictment of the rationalist view of the world is presented through the characters of Brown's intellectual villains, who represent the radical extreme to which the rationalist thinker may sometimes be led. Carwin, Ludloe, and Ormond are clearly identified with much of the radical thought we know Brown became acquainted with in his early reading, and all are engaged to some degree with plans to remake the world and humanity according to rationalist principles. Significantly, all three are clearly villains. Ludloe persecutes Carwin, who himself takes pleasure in dominating the lives of others, and Ormond ruins the life of Helena Cleves and would do the same to Constantia Dudley were he not thwarted before he can accomplish his purpose. Since Brown consistently makes the characters both radical thinkers and obvious villains, it seems certain that he intended the reader to question the value of their principles and to perceive the need for some restraint to be placed on their soaring thoughts and vaunting ambitions.[18] Their minds alone are not sufficient to serve such a purpose, for Carwin and Ormond both reveal themselves capable of self-deception and rationalization.

Other characters, too, by no means so villainous as these, reveal Brown's apparent belief in the ease with which the human mind may deceive itself. The best example, no doubt, is Arthur Mervyn, who starts his career as if he were merely a naive boy at the mercy of evil forces loose in the world but who eventually shows himself to be the master of his environment. The self-deception that Mervyn, perhaps unconsciously, practices is different, however, from that in Carwin or Ormond. Unconcerned with power or dominance over others, Mervyn converts his selfishness into the appearance of benevolence, and by seeming to act on only the best of motives, he succeeds in gaining just what he wants from others. Mervyn maintains the mask of benevolence throughout his career and insists to the end that his motives are unquestionably pure. Readers, however, can see behind the overt actions of the man to the true motivation that lies behind his deeds and thus perceive the deceptions of which human beings are capable.

A similar view is surely presented through the actions of Edgar Huntly, who possesses a number of the qualities already considered. Like Brown's intellectual villains, he has been led into erroneous opinions through the arguments of Waldegrave; like Clara and Theodore Wieland, he is influenced to some extent by the past: his parents' deaths at the hands of the Indians. Like them, too, he attempts to arrive at a just interpretation of what he perceives in the world through his senses, but his inferences, like theirs, are frequently shown to be in error. He shares the false benevolence of Arthur Mervyn, and he sometimes reveals himself to be as compulsive in his actions. Indeed, Huntly would seem to present a most telling attack on the validity of human reasoning were he not also, like Clara Wieland, apparently reclaimed at the end of the book. At any rate, it seems perfectly clear in view of all this evidence that Brown was no naive rationalist by the time he wrote his novels. Reason is still of great value in all of these books and represents the standard in terms of which the aberrations of the characters may be judged. Since all of these characters, however, fall such easy prey to the deceptions of themselves and others, one may surely conclude that Brown placed no blind faith in human reason.

Brown was even more critical of the emotional approach to life, for the characters he drew who follow this path are shown to be even less successful than those who try to guide their lives by reason alone. The highly volatile Stephen Calvert is a case in point, as are the main female characters in his last two novels. Clara Howard believes that she is acting on rational principles, but she, like Jane Talbot, is very much a creature of emotion. None of these characters is capable of consistent action based on rational principle. Each is the prey of any emotion he or she feels and is easily swayed by the influence of others. Stephen Calvert vacillates between his cousin Louisa and Clelia Neville; Jane Talbot is influenced in turn by Mrs. Fielder and Henry Colden. Jane, moreover, falls victim to the emotional appeals of her brother, and Clara Howard gives up her supposedly firm resolves when she hears of Edward's illness and fears that he may die. There can be no question that Brown completely dismisses the emotions as proper guides to conduct.

Brown does not let the matter end here. Indeed, one might argue, he could hardly afford to do so without giving the world over entirely to the nonrational elements in human beings. Convinced of the value of reason, he had of necessity to come to grips with the problem of the many nonrational influences exerted upon the individual and to affirm some standard by which the characters might be kept from falling into error. In *Wieland,* this function is provided, in part at least, by Clara's uncle, a doctor, who tries to help her back to sanity and who at one time explains scientifically the mania that afflicts her brother. The point of view the uncle represents, however, plays no really important part in Brown's subsequent fiction. Rather, Brown seems to affirm yet another element as necessary in one's intellectual makeup if one is to avoid the errors into which both the mind and the passions can lead a person. That element is religion, clearly presented in *Ormond* as the one thing needed by Constantia Dudley to enable her to withstand successfully the evil machinations of her would-be seducer.

Religion is a subject seldom considered of much importance in discussions of Brown,[19] but the vital role it plays in the intellectual drama of *Ormond* justifies a recognition of its influence when it occupies a less obvious place in other of Brown's books. Thus, once aware that the absence of religion is to be seen as a serious flaw in Constantia's education, a reader may certainly consider a similar omission in the training of Clara and Theodore Wieland as equally significant, for the implication is strong that part of the trouble brother and sister experience may derive from this lack. Indeed, even in *Edgar Huntly* there is at least the suggestion that the protagonist is influenced by the irreligious principles that Waldegrave had instilled in him. Such evidence is by no means strong and might not perhaps be at all convincing did not Brown's final novel, *Jane Talbot,* make abundantly clear his affirmation of the need for religious faith if one is to lead a satisfactory life. It is doubly significant, perhaps, that in this book it is a Godwinian rationalist who is at last converted to religious belief.

Other evidence clearly indicates that Brown turned increasingly to an affirmation of religion as he grew older—so much so that one is tempted to see the depiction of Henry Colden's intellectual development as fundamentally autobiographical.[20] Be that as it may, it is clear that by 1803, Brown openly supported religious values, for, in "The Editors' Address to the Public" in the first issue of the *Literary Magazine,* he expressed his awareness of the bold attacks that had been made on "the foundations of religion and morality" in his times. It was important, he went on to say, that in presenting a magazine to the public, he should explicitly state his policy. "Without equivocation or reserve," he announced himself to be "the ardent friend and the willing champion of the Christian religion," who sought as the reward of his labors the consciousness that he had "in some degree however inconsiderable, contributed to recommend the practice of religious duties."[21] One cannot, of course, apply a passage like this to the books he had written some three to five years earlier, but the statement is significant in revealing the intellectual position toward which he had probably been moving during his writing career.[22]

Because he is concerned with questions of religion in *Wieland,* it seems fair to conclude that by the time he wrote that novel—and certainly as early as *Ormond*—Brown had begun to consider the value of religious faith in the properly regulated life. In none of his fiction is Brown very specific on what that faith should be, though it is clear that it ought not to be the type professed by the two Wielands, father and son. It is obvious, too, that he placed no trust in purely emotional religious feelings, for Jane Talbot's early piety is dismissed as unsubstantial, and he certainly believed that religious faith should have a firm rational basis, for he illustrates in the eventual union of Henry Colden and Jane Talbot the acceptance of both reason and faith which he finally presents as necessary for a successful life. Brown himself was neither a philosopher nor a theologian but a literary artist, and, if he leaves his statement of belief rather vague, that is only to be expected of a man in his time and place and with his intellectual background. In raising the questions he does in his books, however, he sounds a note that was to reecho, in one way or another, in a considerable amount of subsequent American fiction.

James Fenimore Cooper comes immediately to mind. He too, especially in his later novels, became increasingly concerned with questions of reason and faith, and in one, *The Sea Lions,* he presents an action that strongly resembles the end of *Jane Talbot.* Though Cooper may be more specific in expressing his religious views, the basic question is fundamentally the same in both works; the differences merely reflect the personal beliefs of the two men. Much the same conclusion can be drawn from the obvious similarities in theme between Brown's works and those of two other successors, Nathaniel Hawthorne and Herman Melville. The rival claims of head and heart, of reason and emotion, are important concerns of all three, so that Brown may surely be called a forerunner of both men in the development of the concept. Other thematic relations between Brown and subsequent writers can, no doubt, be made, and, though one would not wish by any means to suggest that Brown's importance as a writer can be completely defined by such relations, a perception of them is surely necessary if one is to understand his position in American literature in its full significance.

More important are Brown's claims to attention as a literary artist, for it is, after all, as a novelist and not as a thinker that he must be remembered. His place as a writer of fiction has always been difficult to determine, and because of the faults in his books, it will always be open to question. His novels are all structurally weak. The best of them, it must be admitted, are among the most seriously flawed; *Wieland, Edgar Huntly,* and *Arthur Mervyn* fall far short of being clearly organized and well-integrated books. Indeed, only *Jane Talbot* and *Ormond* approach the structural unity the twentieth-century critic demands in fiction. Among his weaknesses, too, must be added the defective style, with its inappropriate words and involved circumlocutions, the thinness of his descriptions of the physical setting, and the lack of dimension in some of his characters. With such serious flaws as these, one might ask, how can his novels survive? They seem to be weak in all of those elements generally considered to be essential in all good fiction.

The answer is simply that in each of these areas, Brown displays qualities that more than make up for his faults. Though each of his better novels, taken as a whole, is structurally flawed, each also contains long and important stretches in which the action moves forward with a pace and an interest that completely absorb the reader. The handling of the subplot in *Wieland* is indefensible, yet readers quickly forget it once they become involved in the problems of Clara Wieland and in the suspenseful main events of the story, which move with an inexorable sweep toward the denouement. The same is true of *Edgar Huntly.* Clithero's account of his past and Weymouth's digression are discordant notes in the basic tone of the book, yet the compelling episodes of Huntly's thrilling and significant frontier adventures carry the novel forward to a strong and meaningful conclusion. In like manner, the chaotic second part of *Arthur Mervyn* cannot entirely detract from the rather well-rounded and fascinating story Brown tells in the first. In each of these books, major parts of the action reveal an artistic talent in the author that is not as apparent in the novel as a whole. So important are the major episodes, however, that the books can be read and enjoyed for the artistic value of those dominant, well-presented parts.

A similar judgment can be made on Brown's style. Though it is not at all difficult to find in his books examples of his writing that are clearly ludicrous, such defects are not really so serious as they seem to be when the sentences are pulled out of context and viewed in isolation. Brown is, of course, no great stylist, but, in his three best books, the style serves as a suitable vehicle for the action presented. One can believe in Clara Wieland's distraught language, overdone though it may sometimes be, for it fits her character and predicament. One perceives the irony apparent in Mervyn's account of his life and accepts the portrayal of Huntly's compulsive actions because the language in which the characters analyze their motives and recount their deeds is, for all its faults, fundamentally convincing. The descriptions, too, weak though they certainly are in the broader aspects of setting, manage to hold the reader in many specific episodes, like Clara Wieland's confrontation of the danger in her closet, Arthur Mervyn's experiences during the plague in Philadelphia, or Edgar Huntly's adventures near the elm tree or deep in the cave. These scenes have a reality and an immediacy that can only be attributed to Brown's skill in handling the language.

In characterization, too, Brown shows considerable artistic talent. One does not know what his characters look like, and even some of the major ones are not very well presented. Wieland, for example, remains rather flat throughout much of the book, and Ormond ends up a melodramatic villain. Yet faults like these are more than overbalanced by the psychological validity that his best characters undoubtedly possess. The descent into madness of Clara Wieland and Edgar Huntly is convincingly depicted, and although one may know little about their external appearance, the reason for their existence in the story—the psychological aberration—is effectively drawn. Arthur Mervyn, in his apparently unconscious duplicity, possesses a psychological reality that is unforgettable; Wieland, in his speech to the court, is a believable maniac; and minor characters, like Carwin or Helena

Cleves, have an individual quality about them that prevents their becoming only flat representations of intellectual or emotional states. Even Constantia Dudley, despite her collapse at the end of *Ormond,* shows a feminine charm that makes her believable. In the minor novels, Jane Talbot stands out as a character whose intellectual and emotional conflicts are particularly well depicted.

Yet whatever his strengths and weaknesses may have been in conventional characterization, Brown is best remembered for the revelation of character he achieved in *Wieland* and *Edgar Huntly* through the use of such Gothic devices as the enclosure, the journey through a labyrinth, and the psychological double. The temple, the summerhouse, and Clara's room and closet in *Wieland* function as symbols of mind through which the mental state of Clara—and, indeed, of other major characters—is revealed. And Edgar Huntly's pursuit of Clithero, his psychological double, through the labyrinth of Norwalk, his descent into the cave, and his tortuous return through the wilderness to civilization and presumably to sanity are all effective means for portraying a psychological development in the character that could not be so well presented through the conventional methods of characterization. Brown's use of these Gothic devices to reveal the psychological state of these characters was an important innovation in American fiction that has borne significant fruit in the works of subsequent writers. It also gave his most important books a special appeal that has made them so memorable to readers from his generation to ours. It was without question his major achievement.

Taken on balance, therefore, the novels of Charles Brockden Brown are by no means so poor as a simple enumeration of their faults might seem to indicate. Overriding the major flaws are strengths that clearly reveal the undeniable genius of the author. He could tell an absorbing, suspenseful story through the actions of psychologically believable characters, and, at the same time, he could make the physical movement of the plot the vehicle for an intellectual drama that has an interest of its own. At the levels of both action and theme, the novels generate an intellectual and emotional power that raises them above the level of mere forerunners of later and better fiction. Their historical significance, of course, is unquestioned, but it must not be overemphasized. In his brief career as a novelist, Charles Brockden Brown initiated a kind of fiction that was to become an important type in subsequent American literature. At the same time, he created in the best parts of his better novels—*Wieland, Edgar Huntly,* and *Arthur Mervyn*—a body of work that can still be read with considerable pleasure today.

Notes and References

Quotations from Brown's major works are from the bicentennial edition of *The Novels and Related Works of Charles Brockden Brown,* ed. Sydney J. Krause et al. (Kent, Ohio: Kent State University Press, 1977–87). Citations in the text are to volume and page numbers in this edition.

Chapter One

1. For the poem, see Harry R. Warfel, *Charles Brockden Brown: American Gothic Novelist* (Gainesville: University of Florida Press, 1949), 32–33; for the essays, entitled "The Rhapsodist," see Charles Brockden Brown, *The Rhapsodist and Other Uncollected Writings,* ed. Harry R. Warfel (New York: Scholars' Facsimiles & Reprints, 1943), 1–24.

2. Richard Chase, *The American Novel and Its Tradition* (Garden City, N.Y.: Doubleday, 1957), 37.

3. R. W. B. Lewis, *The American Adam: Innocence, Tragedy, and Tradition in the Nineteenth Century* (Chicago: University of Chicago Press, 1955), 92.

4. See the references to Brown and his novels in the following: *The Letters of John Keats,* ed. Hyder E. Rollins (Cambridge, Mass.: Harvard University Press, 1958), 2:173; (for Shelley) Thomas Love Peacock, *Works,* ed. Henry Cole (London: Bentley, 1875), 3:409–10; James Fenimore Cooper, *Notions of the Americans: Picked Up by a Travelling Bachelor* (Philadelphia: Carey, Lea, and Carey, 1828), 2:110–11; Edgar Allan Poe, *Works,* ed. James A. Harrison (New York: DeFau, 1902), 11:206, 12:224, 249, 16:41; William Hickling Prescott, "Memoir of Charles Brockden Brown, the American Novelist," *Biographical and Critical Miscellanies* (Philadelphia: Lippincott, 1865), 1–56; Nathaniel Hawthorne, *Works,* centenary edition, ed. William Charvat et al. (Columbus: Ohio State University Press, 1964–), 10:174, 380; John Greenleaf Whittier, *Works* (Boston: Houghton Mifflin, 1892), 7:392–95; Margaret Fuller, *Writings,* ed. Mason Wade (New York: Viking, 1941), 374, 377–80.

5. George Dixon Snell, *The Shapers of American Fiction, 1798–1947* (New York: E. P. Dutton, 1947), 39, 44.

6. Leslie A. Fiedler, *Love and Death in the American Novel* (New York: Criterion Books, 1960), 143.

7. Martin S. Vilas, *Charles Brockden Brown: A Study of Early American Fiction* (Burlington, Vt.: Free Press Association, 1904), 27.

8. Paul Witherington, "Brockden Brown's Other Novels: *Clara Howard* and *Jane Talbot,*" *Nineteenth-Century Fiction* 29 (1974):257.

9. Disagreements about Mervyn's character are conveniently summarized

by Norman S. Grabo in his "Historical Essay" in the bicentennial edition of *Arthur Mervyn,* 3:474–75. See also chapter 4.

10. David Lee Clark, *Charles Brockden Brown: Pioneer Voice of America* (Durham, N.C.: Duke University Press, 1952), 192; Alexander Cowie, *The Rise of the American Novel* (New York: American, 1951), 91.

11. Warfel, *Brown,* 9; Lewis, *American Adam,* 95–96. Both cite passages from *Arthur Mervyn* in support of their opinions.

12. Clark, *Brown,* 37. Warfel, *Brown,* 36, however, dates his withdrawal from the study of law in 1792. See also Robert A. Ferguson, *Law and Letters in American Culture* (Cambridge, Mass.: Harvard University Press, 1984), 129–30.

13. Warfel, *Brown,* 37–38.

14. Ibid., 7, 26–27.

15. Ibid., 17.

16. Herbert Brown, "Charles Brockden Brown's 'The Story of Julius': Rousseau and Richardson 'Improved'," in *Essays Mostly on Periodical Publishing in America,* ed. James Woodress (Durham N.C.: Duke University Press, 1973), 35–53. See also Sydney J. Krause, "*Clara Howard* and *Jane Talbot*: Godwin on Trial," in *Critical Essays on Charles Brockden Brown,* ed. Bernard Rosenthal (Boston: G. K. Hall, 1981), 188–96.

17. Warfel, *Brown,* 54–55.

18. *The Diary of Elihu Hubbard Smith (1771–1798),* ed. James E. Cronin (Philadelphia: American Philosophical Society, 1973), 171.

19. For a discussion of the New York Friendly Club and Brown's relation to it, see James E. Cronin, "Elihu Hubbard Smith and the New York Friendly Club, 1795–1798," *PMLA* 64 (1949):471–79.

20. *Diary of Elihu Hubbard Smith,* 439.

21. Charles Brockden Brown, *Alcuin: A Dialogue,* with an afterword by Lee R. Edwards (New York: Grossman, 1971).

22. For a full discussion of the composition and publication of all parts of *Alcuin,* see Robert D. Arner, "Historical Essay" in the bicentennial edition of *Alcuin* and *Memoirs of Stephen Calvert,* 6:273–78.

23. Cathy N. Davidson, "The Matter and Manner of Charles Brockden Brown's *Alcuin,*" in *Critical Essays on Charles Brockden Brown,* 71–86; Arner, "Historical Essay," 284–86.

24. The letter may be found in Bernard Rosenthal, Introduction to *Critical Essays on Charles Brockden Brown,* 11–16.

25. William Dunlap, *The Life of Charles Brockden Brown: together with Selections from the Rarest of His Printed Works, from His Original Letters, and from His Manuscripts before Unpublished* (Philadelphia: James P. Parke, 1815), 1:70. Cf. Paul Allen, *The Life of Charles Brockden Brown,* Introduction by Charles E. Bennett (Delmar, N.Y.: Scholars' Facsimiles & Reprints, 1975), 70–71.

26. Allen, *Life of Brown,* 71. Dunlap, *Life of Brown,* 1:71, makes no change in this passage.

27. Dunlap, *Life of Brown,* 1:57, 169.

28. A very different view from that expressed here is Ernest Marchand's suggestion that Brown may have put radical opinions into the mouths of his villains so that he could place them before his readers "without bearing the onus of holding them himself." This opinion strikes me as hardly defensible since such a practice would violate all sound principles of both art and propaganda. See Ernest Marchand, Introduction to *Ormond,* by Charles Brockden Brown (New York: American, 1937), xxix.

29. Dunlap, *Life of Brown,* 1:51, 53; Allen, *Life of Brown,* 58, 59. For Wilkins's reaction to Brown's melancholy and other expressions of self-condemnation by Brown, see David Lee Clark, "Unpublished Letters of Charles Brockden Brown and W. W. Wilkins," *University of Texas Studies in English* 27 (1948):84, 102, 103.

30. *Diary of Elihu Hubbard Smith,* 163–64, 170–71.

31. Warfel, *Brown,* 86–88.

32. Dunlap, *Life of Brown,* 1:258. That Brown was a facile writer is also testified to by John Bernard, a British actor who knew him in Philadelphia at the turn of the century. See John Bernard, *Retrospections of America, 1797–1811* (New York: Harper, 1887), 253.

33. See Brown's letter to his brother James, 15 February 1799, quoted in Dunlap, *Life of Brown,* 2:98. Another resume of the plot of *Arthur Mervyn,* thinly disguised with different names, but with little emphasis on the second part, appears in "Walstein's School of History," published in two issues of the *Monthly Magazine and American Review* (August and September–December 1799) and reprinted in Warfel's edition of *The Rhapsodist,* 145–56, esp. 154–56.

34. For additional evidence that Brown may have changed and developed his themes as he wrote, see Larzer Ziff, "A Reading of *Wieland,*" *PMLA* 77 (1962):53–54.

35. W. B. Berthoff, " 'A Lesson on Concealment': Brockden Brown's Method in Fiction," *Philological Quarterly* 37 (1958):45–57, esp. 46–48.

36. Dunlap, *Life of Brown,* 2:16.

37. Although most of it had been printed, the novel was never published because of the sudden death of the publisher and the recalcitrance of his executors. See chapter 5. An "Advertisement" for the book and an "Extract" from it were published in the *Weekly Magazine* in March 1798 and are reprinted in Warfel's edition of *The Rhapsodist,* 135–41.

38. Cf., for example, numbers 4 and 5 of "The Man at Home" (*The Rhapsodist,* ed. Warfel, 47–56), and chapter 7 of *Ormond* (2:63–71).

Chapter Two

1. In addition to those mentioned in note 1 to chapter 1, these include the following, which appeared in the Philadelphia *Weekly Magazine:* the opening chapters of *Arthur Mervyn,* published 16 June–25 August 1798; "The Man at Home," 3 February–28 April 1798; "A Series of Original Letters," 21 April–2 June 1798;

and the "Advertisement" of and an "Extract" from *Sky-Walk,* 17 March and 24 March 1798.

2. A full discussion of the James Yates murders, which are a source for those in *Wieland,* may be found in Alan Axelrod, *Charles Brockden Brown: An American Tale* (Austin: University of Texas Press, 1983), 53–56.

3. Alexander Cowie, "Historical Essay" in the bicentennial edition of *Wieland* and *Memoirs of Carwin the Biloquist,* 1:321–22. Brown's outline may be found in that edition, 1:420–41.

4. Jacob Blanck, *Bibliography of American Literature* (New Haven: Yale University Press, 1955), 1:302.

5. Fred Lewis Pattee, Introduction to *Wieland; or, The Transformation, together with Memoirs of Carwin the Biloquist, a Fragment,* by Charles Brockden Brown (New York: Harcourt, Brace, 1926), xxxvi–xl; Harry R. Warfel, "Charles Brockden Brown's German Sources," *Modern Language Quarterly* 1 (1940):357–65.

6. Axelrod, *Brown,* 61–63; Donald A. Ringe, *American Gothic: Imagination and Reason in Nineteenth-Century Fiction* (Lexington: University Press of Kentucky, 1982), 37–38.

7. See Wayne Franklin, "Tragedy and Comedy in Brown's *Wieland,*" *Novel* 8 (1975):147–63; Michael T. Gilmore, "Calvinism and Gothicism: The Example of Brown's *Wieland,*" *Studies in the Novel* 9 (1977):107–18; Joseph A. Soldati, "The Americanization of Faust: A Study of Charles Brockden Brown's *Wieland,*" *ESQ,* 20 (1974):1–14.

8. This point has been clearly established by Warfel, *Brown,* 107, and by Ziff, "Reading of *Wieland,*" 53–54. Indeed Warfel had observed as early as 1940 that *Wieland* is based on this psychology, citing as a specific source a German novel, Cajetan Tschink's *Geisterseher,* translated as *The Victim of Magical Delusion* (1795), which also makes use of the psychology. Indeed, Warfel cites a long passage from the introduction to the translation that may have influenced Brown's depiction of Wieland as a man who seeks direct communication with God. See "Charles Brockden Brown's German Sources," 361–65.

9. See chapter 1.

10. Brown clearly underscores the "stormy passions" of Pleyel (1:119) not only in this passage but also earlier in the book when Clara mentions "the torments of jealousy" Pleyel undergoes when he fails to get an expected letter from his fiancée in Europe (1:40).

11. Wieland, however, did say shortly before this speech that he is a judge "who is ready to question his own senses when they plead against" her (1:109).

12. Ziff, "Reading of *Wieland,* 53–54. Thomas Pribek, on the other hand, points out that "depravity" had other meanings besides the Calvinistic one in Brown's day and believes that the word should not be construed in the Calvinist sense. See "A Note on 'Depravity' in *Wieland,*" *Philological Quarterly* 64 (1985):273–79.

13. Cf. William M. Manly, "The Importance of Point of View in Brockden

Brown's *Wieland*," *American Literature* 35 (1963):311–21, where Clara is also seen as the central character in the book.

14. Cf. Ziff, "Reading of *Wieland*," 53.

15. Cf. ibid., 53–54. Ziff maintains that the conclusion of the book contradicts the main action by affirming once more at the end the principles of contemporary psychology. For more positive views of the book's conclusion, however, see Norman S. Grabo, *The Coincidental Art of Charles Brockden Brown* (Chapel Hill: University of North Carolina Press, 1981), 23–29, and Cynthia S. Jordan, "On Rereading *Wieland:* 'The Folly of Precipitate Conclusions,' " *Early American Literature* 16 (1981):154–74.

16. In the edition edited by Fred Lewis Pattee in 1926. *Memoirs of Carwin the Biloquist* is also included in the bicentennial edition of *Wieland,* and page numbers in my text are to that edition.

17. Warfel, *Brown,* 104–5; Clark, *Brown,* 168–69. A related view has recently been expressed by Bernard Rosenthal, who reads the book—erroneously, I think—as presenting "the danger of morality based on revealed religion." See Bernard Rosenthal, "The Voices of *Wieland*," in *Critical Essays on Charles Brockden Brown,* 104–25.

18. Cf. Ziff, "Reading of *Wieland*," 54, who maintains that it is easier to explain Wieland's delusion in terms of his lack of religious training than of any "prejudiced expectations." See too his comment (55) that the Wielands' lack of formal education insulated them from sectarian doctrine because the colleges and schools of the time were all religious ones.

19. Ibid., 54, 56.

20. For a full discussion of both the symbols themselves and the relation of Brown's novels to other Gothic fiction, see Donald A. Ringe, "Charles Brockden Brown," in *Major Writers of Early American Literature,* ed. Everett Emerson (Madison: University of Wisconsin Press, 1972), 279–88; Ringe, *American Gothic,* 36–57.

21. See, for example, Pattee, Introduction, xli–xlii; Warfel, *Brown,* 108.

22. Compare, for example, the first few paragraphs of each novel.

23. Brown's use of the multiple point of view in *Wieland* has been noted by Pattee, Introduction, xlii; Warfel, *Brown,* 105–6; and Cowie, *Rise of the American Novel,* 73. Cf. Manly, "Importance of Point of View," 320–21. In addition, Berthoff has observed its recurring use in Brown's fiction. See " 'A Lesson on Concealment,' " 49.

Chapter Three

1. *Diary of Elihu Hubbard Smith,* 460; *Diary of William Dunlap,* in *Collections of the New York Historical Society,* vols. 62–64 (New York: New-York Historical Society, 1930), 335. The three volumes are paged continuously throughout.

2. Cowie, "Historical Essay," 1:336.

3. *Diary of Elihu Hubbard Smith,* 463.

4. *Diary of William Dunlap,* 342.

5. Dunlap, *Life of Brown,* 2:93.

6. Sydney J. Krause, "Historical Notes" in the bicentennial edition of *Ormond,* 2:412–18, 419–21.

7. Dunlap was the first to perceive Brown's use of the Illuminati in *Memoirs of Carwin.* See *Diary of William Dunlap,* 339. See also Ringe, *American Gothic,* 32–33, 38–39.

8. Krause, "Historical Notes," passim.

9. Russel B. Nye, "Historical Essay" in the bicentennial edition of *Ormond,* 2:308–9.

10. The first edition of *Ormond,* on which the bicentennial edition is based, is inconsistent in its handling of proper names. "Constantia" also appears as "Constance" and "Helena" as "Hellen." I am using "Constantia" and "Helena," the names by which the characters have long been known in the scholarship on the book.

11. Cf. Marchand, Introduction, xxix–xxx.

12. Cf. Prescott, "Memoir of Brown," 26, who links Constantia Dudley with Griselda in Chaucer and Boccaccio.

13. Cf. Lillie D. Loshe, *The Early American Novel* (New York: Columbia University Press, 1907), 46; Marchand, Introduction, xxxii–xxxiv.

14. It should be noted, too, that Ormond also uses physical means to influence Constantia, for he helps the Dudley family escape from poverty, and he is instrumental in restoring Dudley his sight (2:280).

15. This was first pointed out by Warfel, *Brown,* 131. He also notes the significance of Constantia's name.

16. This house had once been owned by Stephen Dudley, acquired by Ormond, given to Helena Cleves, and willed to Constantia (2:265–66).

17. Sydney J. Krause, "*Ormond:* Seduction in a New Key," *American Literature* 44 (1973):570–84.

18. Grabo, *Coincidental Art,* 54.

19. Warfel, *Brown,* 131.

20. Marchand, Introduction, xxxii; Warfel, *Brown,* 130, 132–33, as well as a number of more recent critics. A dissenting view may be found in Clark, *Brown,* 173.

21. See the defense of the change in Ormond's behavior quoted in Dunlap, *Life of Brown,* 2:15–16.

22. Paul C. Rodgers, Jr., "Brown's *Ormond:* The Fruits of Improvisation," *American Quarterly* 26 (1974):4–22.

23. Warfel, *Brown,* 137. Cf. Marchand, Introduction, xxxvi, who believes that the Craig episode receives too much emphasis and that both the Baxter story and the early history of Sophia are digressive.

Chapter Four

1. Dunlap, *Life of Brown,* 2:93
2. Norman S. Grabo, "Historical Essay" in the bicentennial edition of *Arthur Mervyn,* 3:453.
3. Ibid., 3:453–55.
4. Ibid., 3:456–57.
5. Dunlap, *Life of Brown,* 2:98.
6. Grabo, "Historical Essay," 3:459–60.
7. See ibid., 3:474–75, and notes 17 and 23.
8. Grabo, "Historical Essay," 3:449.
9. Clark, *Brown,* 180.
10. See, for example, Vilas, *Brown,* 33; Clark, *Brown,* 179. Cowie, *Rise of the American Novel,* 81 also stresses the realism but sees a humanitarian motive behind the descriptions.
11. Lewis, *American Adam,* 97, 92–93; W. B. Berthoff, "Adventures of the Young Man: An Approach to Charles Brockden Brown," *American Quarterly* 9 (1957):426–28.
12. This concept is the whole point of ibid., esp. 425. See also Lewis, *American Adam,* 97–98.
13. Mervyn comes from a family of children almost all of whom have died "as they attained the age of nineteen or twenty" (One sister, we later learn, committed suicide after being seduced). He believes, therefore, that he may reasonably anticipate "the same premature fate" (3:17), a belief Berthoff sees as the motivating factor in Mervyn's eager grasping for life. See "Adventures of the Young Man," 430. Mervyn does not succumb to this fate, but his belief renders plausible his later return to Philadelphia during the plague.
14. Wallace, it should be noted, turns out to be the same young man who gulled him on his first night in the city (3:166–67, 175).
15. Dunlap, *Life of Brown,* 2:97–98.
16. Cf. W. B. Berthoff, Introduction to *Arthur Mervyn; or, Memoirs of the Year 1793,* by Charles Brockden Brown (New York: Holt, Rinehart and Winston, 1962), xvi.
17. In addition to Berthoff, ibid., xvii, see Patrick Branccacio, "Studied Ambiguities: *Arthur Mervyn* and the Problem of the Unreliable Narrator," *American Literature* 42 (1970):18–27; Michael Davitt Bell, " 'The Double-Tongued Deceiver': Sincerity and Duplicity in the Novels of Charles Brockden Brown," *Early American Literature* 9 (1974):155–58; and Emory Elliott, "Narrative Unity and Moral Resolution in *Arthur Mervyn,*" in *Critical Essays on Charles Brockden Brown,* 142–63.
18. The shift of Mervyn's affection from Eliza Hadwin to Achsa Fielding has several times been commented on by readers. Dunlap, *Life of Brown,* 2:40, felt that Eliza was abandoned "in a manner as unexpected as disgusting," and Peacock, *Works,* 3:409, reports that Shelley was displeased with the shift and concluded

from it that Brown wanted to bring his book "to an uncomfortable conclusion." For more recent comments, see, among others, Berthoff, "Adventures of the Young Man," 432; Grabo, *Coincidental Art,* 109–11, 117–20.

19. That Mervyn himself is psychologically uneasy with his successful marriage is perhaps revealed near the end of the book by a fit of sleepwalking and by the dream he has in which he is stabbed in the breast by the dead Mr. Fielding. Mervyn, however, does not allow such thoughts or actions to disturb him for long. See Berthoff, "Adventures of the Young Man," 432. The episode has been much commented on by critics of a Freudian persuasion. See, for example, Axelrod, *Brown,* 140–42.

20. Berthoff, Introduction, xvii.

21. Ibid., xvii.

22. Ibid., xviii.

23. Grabo, *Coincidental Art,* 126. Other favorable views of Mervyn's character may be found in Lewis, *American Adam,* 98; Kenneth Bernard, "*Arthur Mervyn:* The Ordeal of Innocence," *Texas Studies in Literature and Language* 6 (1965):441–59; and James H. Justus, "Arthur Mervyn, American," *American Literature* 42 (1970):304–24. Two recent critics have taken a more neutral view of Mervyn and his experiences. See Daniel A. Cohen, "Arthur Mervyn and His Elders: The Ambivalence of Youth in the Early Republic," *William and Mary Quarterly,* 3d ser. 43 (1986):362–80, and Cathy N. Davidson, *Revolution and the Word: The Rise of the Novel in America* (New York: Oxford University Press, 1986), 239–53.

24. "Walstein's School of History" may be conveniently found in *The Rhapsodist,* ed. Warfel, 145–56.

25. Grabo, *Coincidental Art,* 125–27.

26. Cf. Berthoff, "Adventures of the Young Man," 433–34.

27. Cf. Berthoff, Introduction, xviii.

28. Cf. Lewis, *American Adam,* 96.

Chapter Five

1. Sydney J. Krause, "Historical Essay" in the bicentennial edition of *Edgar Huntly,* 4:298–302.

2. Dunlap, *Life of Brown,* 1:259.

3. Krause, "Historical Essay," 4:308.

4. Ibid., 4:305–17.

5. Ibid., 4:372–77. *Maria Kittle* had also been published serially in 1790–91.

6. Brown had, however, created two characters who had withdrawn to the wilderness: the Rhapsodist, who lived on the banks of the Ohio (*The Rhapsodist,* ed. Warfel, 13–15), and Stephen Calvert, who moved to the shores of Lake Michigan to avoid the "temptation and calamity" of society (6:71–72). In neither case does Brown make much use of the material.

7. John Neal, *American Writers: A Series of Papers Contributed to Black-*

wood's Magazine (1824–1825), ed. Fred Lewis Pattee (Durham, N.C.: Duke University Press, 1937), 68. Cf. Lulu Rumsey Wiley, *The Sources and Influence of the Novels of Charles Brockden Brown* (New York: Scarecrow Press, 1950), 215–17; Warfel, *Brown,* 155; Cowie, *Rise of the American Novel,* 85; Chase, *American Novel,* 36; Fiedler, *Love and Death in the American Novel,* 140. Cooper criticizes *Edgar Huntly* in his preface to the 1821 edition of *The Spy.*

8. Warfel, *Brown,* 155.

9. Brown's use of landscape as symbol has been much commented on. See, for example, Kenneth Bernard, "Charles Brockden Brown and the Sublime," *Personalist* 45 (1964):235–49; Richard F. Fleck, "Symbolic Landscapes in *Edgar Huntly,*" *Research Studies* (Washington State University) 39 (1971):229–32; Philip Russell Hughes, "Archetypal Patterns in *Edgar Huntly,*" *Studies in the Novel* 5 (1973):176–90; and George Toles, "Charting the Hidden Landscape: *Edgar Huntly,*" *Early American Literature* 16 (1981):133–53. For a different view of Brown's use of the landscape, see Dennis Berthold, "Charles Brockden Brown, *Edgar Huntly,* and the Origins of the American Picturesque," *William and Mary Quarterly* 3d ser. 41 (1984):62–84.

10. Cf. Fiedler, *Love and Death in the American Novel,* 147, who sees "the cave as a metaphor for the mysteries of the human heart."

11. It should be noted in passing that, as Warfel, *Brown,* 161, observes, the Weymouth-Waldegrave relationship parallels in one respect the Mrs. Lorimer-Wiatte one, in that Weymouth, like Mrs. Lorimer, believes that his life is inseparably tied up with that of another, in his case, Waldegrave.

12. Cf. Fiedler, *Love and Death in the American Novel,* 143.

13. Cf. Cowie, *Rise of the American Novel,* 84.

14. This is the second symbolic death that Huntly undergoes.

15. This is Huntly's third symbolic death, for those who shoot at him are certain that he has perished in the water.

16. Cf. Warfel, *Brown,* 160, who believes that Huntly's madness is the same as that of the two Wielands.

17. Though Waldegrave's letters do indeed contribute to Huntly's irrational actions, Huntly seems more concerned with his failure to comply with his friend's wishes than with his own intellectual or moral state.

18. That the cave scene is a possible source for Poe's story has been argued in David Lee Clark, "The Sources of Poe's 'The Pit and the Pendulum,' " *Modern Language Notes* 44 (1929):349–56.

19. Cf. Cowie, *Rise of the American Novel,* 84, who also believes that Brown's work in the frontier scenes need not "be accounted any less successful than Poe's."

20. For extended discussions of the double in *Edgar Huntly,* see Kenneth Bernard, "*Edgar Huntly:* Charles Brockden Brown's Unsolved Murder," *Library Chronicle* 33 (1967):30–53; Krause, "Historical Essay," 4:317–30. A more general

discussion of the use of doubling in Brown's works may be found in Grabo, *Coincidental Art,* 160–85.

Chapter Six

1. *Diary of Elihu Hubbard Smith,* 463; *Diary of William Dunlap,* 335–36.

2. Arner, "Historical Essay," 6:298–301; S. W. Reid, "Textual Essay" in the bicentennial edition of *Alcuin* and *Memoirs of Stephen Calvert,* 6:357–58.

3. Berthoff, "Adventures of the Young Man," 422.

4. See especially the scene in which Sydney encounters the real Felix and mistakes him for his twin (6:266–70).

5. Felix and Stephen are shown to have different colored hair and eyes, and Stephen has a scar, which puzzles Clelia at one point because she does not remember having noticed it before (6:214–16, 269).

6. Cf. Berthoff, "Adventures of the Young Man," 424–25.

7. Cf. ibid., 422.

8. See Grabo, *Coincidental Art,* 149, 157; and Arner, "Historical Essay," 6:306. Arner's interpretation, however, requires us to look at the book through the prism of Freudian psychology.

9. See Warfel, *Brown,* 188–89; and Charles E. Bennett, "Charles Brockden Brown: Man of Letters," in *Critical Essays on Charles Brockden Brown,* 212.

10. For evidence of Brown's movements in 1800 and his settlement in Philadelphia, see Donald A. Ringe, "Historical Essay" in the bicentennial edition of *Clara Howard* and *Jane Talbot,* 5:437n6.

11. Dunlap, *Life of Brown,* 2:100.

12. See Ringe, "Historical Essay," 5:434–35.

13. For a full discussion of the composition and publication of Clara Howard, see ibid., 5:436–42.

14. Clark, *Brown,* 182. Cf. Warfel, *Brown,* 192; Loshe, *Early American Novel,* 46. Both see Clara as similar to Constantia.

15. Krause, "*Clara Howard* and *Jane Talbot,*" 187–91, 198–202, 208.

16. Whoever prepared the British edition of 1807 must have read the book in these terms, for he changed the name of the hero to Philip Stanley and the title of the book to *Philip Stanley; or, The Enthusiasm of Love.* The name of the character and the subtitle were used in subsequent American editions, which appeared as *Clara Howard; or, The Enthusiasm of Love,* but they are not authorial and have no textual significance. The bicentennial edition, which I follow, has restored both the name and the title to those of the first American edition.

17. For a full discussion of the composition and publication of *Jane Talbot,* see Ringe, "Historical Essay," 5:443–51.

18. Krause, "*Clara Howard* and *Jane Talbot,*" 186, 188–89, 199, 202–8.

19. Krause, in ibid., 186, has pointed out, however, that "in Mrs. Fielder's

oft-quoted complaint against Colden, it is not so much Godwin who is being arraigned as the anti-social radicalism which was synonymous with his name."

20. Cf. Warfel, *Brown,* 199–200.

21. Cf. ibid., 198–99.

22. A statement of the importance of the concept in both Hawthorne and Melville may be found in F. O. Matthiessen, *American Renaissance: Art and Expression in the Age of Emerson and Whitman* (New York: Oxford University Press, 1941), 345.

23. For a discussion of the critical reception of both *Clara Howard* and *Jane Talbot,* see Ringe, "Historical Essay," 5:452–71.

24. Robert E. Hemenway and Joseph Katz, Introduction to Paul Allen, *The Late Charles Brockden Brown* (Columbia, S.C.: J. Faust, 1976), li–lv. Like other critics, however, they believe that Brown was at his best in the Gothic romances.

25. Witherington, "Brockden Brown's Other Novels," 257–72.

Chapter Seven

1. Minor works in *The Monthly Magazine* written by Brown or attributed to him include: "Thessalonica: A Roman Story" (May 1799), "Portrait of an Emigrant" (June 1799), "A Lesson on Concealment; or, Memoirs of Mary Selwyn" (March 1800), "The Trials of Arden" (July 1800), "Friendship: An Original Letter" (July 1800), "The Household: A Fragment" (August 1800), "Original Letters" (August 1800). Cf. Carl Van Doren, "Minor Tales of Brockden Brown, 1798–1800," *Nation* 100 (1915):46–47; Warfel, *Brown,* 175–76; Clark, *Brown,* 133–34. Van Doren points out, moreover, that "Original Letters" are part of the same story as the "Jessica" fragment, printed in Dunlap. See also note 2.

2. These are "Jessica" 1:108–69; "Dialogues" (on music and painting), 2:122–39; "Signior Adini," 2:140–69; "The Scribbler," 2:264–73. The first and third are unnamed in Dunlap, *Life of Brown.* "Thessalonica" is also reprinted here (2:170–99), and "Friendship" appears as part of "Jessica" (1:120–24). There is also in Allen, *Life of Brown,* 222–242, an unnamed "Harry Wallace," which Dunlap did not include in his book.

3. This story, a narrative of Cicero's death told by a faithful retainer, comprises a separately numbered forty-eight pages at the end of volume 3 in the second edition, 1799. See Blanck, 1:304.

4. Berthoff, " 'A Lesson on Concealment,' " 47–48, 55–57.

5. W. B. Berthoff, "Charles Brockden Brown's Historical 'Sketches': A Consideration," *American Literature* 28 (1956):149. For much of the interpretation that follows in this paragraph, I am indebted to Berthoff's article, esp. 150–54.

6. Dunlap, *Life of Brown,* 1:170–258, 262–396. Cf. Allen, *Life of Brown,* 170–222, 242–358. Each includes material that is not in the other. Additional fragments appear in three issues of the *Literary Magazine.* For a discussion of all these fragments, see Bennett, "Charles Brockden Brown," 219–20, 223.

7. Cf. Warfel, *Brown,* 71–72.

8. Berthoff, "Charles Brockden Brown's Historical 'Sketches,' " 150, 153–54. See also his "Brockden Brown: The Politics of a Man of Letters," *Serif* 3 (1966):3–11.

9. He did, however, begin a tragedy on "an imaginary incident of Egyptian history" and completed two acts, which he subsequently burned. See Bernard, *Retrospections of America,* 254–55.

10. For a full discussion of Brown's translation, see Cecelia Tichi, "Charles Brockden Brown, Translator," *American Literature* 44 (1972):1–12. Volney's book in the Brown translation has been republished with an introduction by George W. White (New York: Hafner, 1968).

11. Clark, *Brown,* 261, argues that this pamphlet is not by Brown, although it is ascribed to him by Dunlap, *Life of Brown,* 2:69–74.

12. Warfel, *Brown,* 222, mentions only the *Memoirs of Carwin.* Alfred Weber ascribes to Brown the short story "Somnambulism: A Fragment," which appeared in the issue for May 1805. See Alfred Weber, "Eine neu entdeckte Kurzgeschichte C. B. Browns," *Jahrbuch für Amerikastudien* 8 (1963):280–96. Clark ascribes to Brown the five-part story "Omar and Fatima; or, The Apothecary of Ispahan," which appeared between July and December 1807. See Clark, *Brown,* 228. See also Charles Brockden Brown, *Somnambulism and Other Stories,* ed. with an introduction and critical notes by Alfred Weber (Frankfurt am Main: Peter Lang, 1987).

13. Of this work, only the prospectus has survived; the manuscript was lost after Brown's death. See Warfel, *Brown,* 234.

14. "The Editors' Address to the Public," *Literary Magazine and American Register* 1 (1803):4. The principal reason for this opinion, he goes on to say, is that while time enlarges and refines a man's powers, the world judges his mature "capacities and principles" from what he wrote as a youth (5).

15. Although most accounts of Brown's life give 22 February 1810 as his death date, in the footnotes to his biography, privately distributed in Dittoed form in 1953, Warfel cites references that Brown died on 21 February and was buried the following day.

16. Clark, *Brown,* 192, Warfel, *Brown,* 108–9, 136–37, 147–48, 162–63, 200–201.

17. Berthoff, " 'A Lesson on Concealment,' " 46–47.

18. For the often quoted passage in which Brown discusses the use of such characters in fiction, see the "Advertisement" for *Sky-Walk,* printed in *The Rhapsodist,* ed. Warfel, 136. Cf. Clark, *Brown,* 164–65, 171, 173, 181, 183, who makes much of this passage in his criticism of some of the novels.

19. A notable exception is Warfel, *Brown,* 100–102, 130–31, 136, 198–200, who treats the subject in his discussions not only of *Wieland* but also of *Ormond* and *Jane Talbot.* For a contrasting view, see Clark, *Brown,* 168–69, 173.

20. Cf. Warfel, *Brown,* 200, who suggests that Brown's association with John Blair Linn, a minister, may be reflected in this novel.

21. "The Editors' Address to the Public," 5.

22. Additional evidence of Brown's increasing conservatism is provided by the historical "Sketches," a major portion of which, Berthoff conjectures, dates from about this time and later. See "Charles Brockden Brown's Historical 'Sketches,' " 147–54. We cannot, however, apply the material in the "Sketches" to the novels, any more than we can the passage from the *Literary Magazine.*

Selected Bibliography

PRIMARY WORKS

This bibliography contains the first editions of Brown's books and pamphlets, including collections of his short pieces, and the most recent and reliable edition of his novels and related works. A number of Brown's short pieces and fragments are also referred to in the Notes and References. More information on the first editions may be found in Jacob Blanck, *Bibliography of American Literature* (New Haven: Yale University Press, 1955–), 1:302–9; and Sydney J. Krause, with the assistance of Jane Nieset, "A Census of the Works of Charles Brockden Brown," *Serif* 3 (1966):27–55.

First Editions

Alcuin: A Dialogue. New York: Printed by T. and J. Swords, 1798. Parts 1 and 2 only; parts 3 and 4 were printed in William Dunlap, *The Life of Charles Brockden Brown* (Philadelphia: James P. Parke, 1815), 1:71–105, and as "The Paradise of Women" in the English abridgement of Dunlap's biography, *Memoirs of Charles Brockden Brown, the American Novelist* (London: Henry Colburn, 1822), 247–308.

Wieland; or, The Transformation. An American Tale. New York: Printed by T. and J. Swords, for H. Caritat, 1798.

Ormond; or, The Secret Witness. New York: Printed by G. Forman, for H. Caritat, 1799.

Arthur Mervyn; or, Memoirs of the Year 1793. Philadelphia: Printed and Published by H. Maxwell, 1799.

Edgar Huntly; or, Memoirs of a Sleep-Walker. Philadelphia: Printed by H. Maxwell, 1799.

Arthur Mervyn; or, Memoirs of the Year 1793. Second Part. New York: Printed and Sold by George F. Hopkins, 1800.

Clara Howard; In a Series of Letters. Philadelphia: Asbury Dickins, 1801. Published in England as *Philip Stanley; or, The Enthusiasm of Love.* London: Lane, Newman, 1807. In nineteenth-century American editions of Brown's collected novels, it was entitled *Clara Howard; or, The Enthusiasm of Love.*

Jane Talbot: A Novel. Philadelphia: John Conrad; Baltimore: M. and J. Conrad; Washington City: Rapin, Conrad, 1801.

An Address to the Government of the United States, on the Cession of Louisiana to the

French; and on the Late Breach of Treaty by the Spaniards: Including the Translation of a Memorial, on the War of St. Domingo, and Cession of the Missisippi [*sic*] *to France, Drawn Up by a French Counsellor of State*. Philadelphia: John Conrad; Baltimore: M. and J. Conrad; Washington City: Rapin, Conrad, 1803.

Monroe's Embassy, or, the Conduct of the Government, in Relation to Our Claims to the Navigation of the Missisippi [*sic*], *Considered*. Philadelphia: John Conrad; Baltimore: M. and J. Conrad; Washington City: Rapin, Conrad, 1803.

The British Treaty. N.p., n.d. [Philadelphia, 1807] Attributed to Brown by William Dunlap, *The Life of Charles Brockden Brown* (Philadelphia: James P. Parke, 1815), 2:69–74.

An Address to the Congress of the United States, on the Utility and Justice of Restrictions upon Foreign Commerce. With Reflections on Foreign Trade in General, and the Future Prospects of America. Philadelphia: C. & A. Conrad, 1809.

Carwin, the Biloquist, and Other American Tales and Pieces. London: Henry Colburn, 1822. Brown's two most important fragments, included in this edition, *Memoirs of Carwin the Biloquist,* and *Memoirs of Stephen Calvert,* had already been printed in William Dunlap, *The Life of Charles Brockden Brown* (Philadelphia: James P. Parke, 1815), 2:200–63, 274–472.

The Rhapsodist and Other Uncollected Writings. Edited by Harry R. Warfel. New York: Scholars' Facsimiles & Reprints, 1943.

Somnambulism and Other Stories. Edited, with an Introduction and Critical Notes, by Alfred Weber. Frankfurt am Main: Peter Lang, 1987.

Collected Edition

The Novels and Related Works of Charles Brockden Brown. Bicentennial edition. Edited by Sydney J. Krause et al. Six vol. Kent, Ohio: Kent State University Press, 1977–87. Supersedes all other editions. Each volume presents a well-edited text and contains both a historical and a textual essay.

SECONDARY WORKS

This section cites the major biographies, the most recent bibliographies, and those critical works that are likely to be most useful to the general student. Other books and articles are cited in the Notes and References. More recent items may be found in the annual bibliography in *PMLA* and the volumes of *American Literary Scholarship: An Annual* (published by Duke University Press), where selected items are discussed and evaluated.

Biographies

Allen, Paul. *The Life of Charles Brockden Brown.* Introduction by Charles E. Bennett. Delmar, N.Y.: Scholars' Facsimiles & Reprints, 1975. A facsimile reproduction of the volume prepared by Allen, one copy of which was printed but never published. It was revised by William Dunlap (see below). Allen's book has also been reproduced as *The Late Charles Brockden Brown.* Introduction by Robert E. Hemenway and Joseph Katz. Columbia, S.C.: J. Faust, 1976. The texts of the two reproductions are identical.

Clark, David Lee. *Charles Brockden Brown: Pioneer Voice of America.* Durham, N.C.: Duke University Press, 1952. Reprints material not readily available elsewhere but devotes relatively little space to criticism of the novels, the treatment of which is sometimes inaccurate and strongly colored by Clark's view of Brown as a proponent of radical ideas.

Dunlap, William. *The Life of Charles Brockden Brown: together with Selections from the Rarest of His Printed Works, from His Original Letters, and from His Manuscripts Before Unpublished.* Philadelphia: James P. Parke, 1815. Vol. 1 is Dunlap's revision of Paul Allen's work (see above); vol. 2 is Dunlap's own. Though inaccurate and disorganized, it is the basis for all subsequent studies of Brown and is particularly valuable for the reprinting of some of Brown's letters and fragments. It was abridged as *Memoirs of Charles Brockden Brown, the American Novelist.* London: Henry Colburn, 1822.

Warfel, Harry R. *Charles Brockden Brown: American Gothic Novelist.* Gainesville: University of Florida Press, 1949. The most reliable, useful, and readable of the biographies, clearly organized and presented; contains judicious criticism of the novels.

Bibliographies

Carpenter, Charles A. "Selective Bibliography of Writings about Charles Brockden Brown." In *Critical Essays on Charles Brockden Brown.* Edited by Bernard Rosenthal. Boston: G. K. Hall, 1981. Lists general critical works by period of composition; specific studies by the works under discussion.

Parker, Patricia L. *Charles Brockden Brown: A Reference Guide.* Boston: G. K. Hall, 1980. An annotated bibliography that lists writings about Brown in one chronological order from 1796 to 1978.

Criticism

Axelrod, Alan. *Charles Brockden Brown: An American Tale.* Austin: University of Texas Press, 1983. Discusses Brown as a specifically American writer by examining the tension "between the Old World and the New" in his fiction.

Bell, Michael Davitt. *The Development of American Romance: The Sacrifice of Relation.* Chicago: University of Chicago Press, 1980. Sees at the center of Brown's four main novels a dialectic between innocence and experience, sincerity and duplicity, that has philosophical, psychological, political, and literary implications.

Berthoff, W. B. "Adventures of the Young Man: An Approach to Charles Brockden Brown." *American Quarterly* 9 (1957):421–34. Considers *Edgar Huntly, Stephen Calvert,* and *Arthur Mervyn* as stories of initiation but treats only *Arthur Mervyn* and, to a lesser extent, *Stephen Calvert* in detail.

———. " 'A Lesson on Concealment': Brockden Brown's Method in Fiction." *Philological Quarterly* 37 (1958):45–57. Describes Brown's fictional method as a means for testing ideas in terms of human motives and actions and illustrates its contention through an analysis of one of Brown's short stories.

———. "Charles Brockden Brown's Historical 'Sketches': A Consideration." *American Literature* 28 (1956):147–54. Argues that a major portion of the "Sketches" was probably written much later than had generally been supposed and interprets them as basically conservative documents.

Chase, Richard. *The American Novel and Its Tradition.* New York: Doubleday, 1957. Good discussions of *Wieland* and *Edgar Huntly* but more important for its treatment of Brown as a forerunner, in his use of melodrama, of a major strain in the American novel.

Cohen, Daniel A. "Arthur Mervyn and His Elders: The Ambivalence of Youth in the Early Republic." *William and Mary Quarterly* 3d ser. 43 (1986):362–80. Suggests that the apparent inconsistencies in Arthur Mervyn's character may be clarified if his career is seen in terms of the economic and social instability of the early national period.

Critical Essays on Charles Brockden Brown. Edited by Bernard Rosenthal. Boston: G. K. Hall, 1981. Six nineteenth-century reviews and early critical essays, eight original essays by twentieth-century critics, and a selective bibliography of books and articles on Brown and his works.

Davidson, Cathy N. *Revolution and the Word: The Rise of the Novel in America.* New York: Oxford University Press, 1986. Sees the meaning of *Arthur Mervyn* as ambiguous because "two radically different stories" are latent in the novel, both of which "are possible in the nation which the text evokes."

Davis, David Brion. *Homicide in American Fiction, 1798–1860: A Study in Social Values.* Ithaca, N.Y.: Cornell University Press, 1957. Discusses *Wieland* and *Edgar Huntly* at some length but leans rather heavily on modern psychological theory in interpreting them.

Elliott, Emory. "Charles Brockden Brown, 1771–1810." In *American Writers, A Collection of Literary Biographies,* supp. 1, pt. 1. Edited by Leonard Unger. New York: Charles Scribner's Sons, 1979. A survey of Brown's life and work that presents the novels as designed to appeal to both a popular and an intellectual audience.

———. *Revolutionary Writers: Literature and Authority in the New Republic, 1725–1810.* New York: Oxford University Press, 1982. Reprints some of the material from his earlier essay but adds a long discussion of *Arthur Mervyn* as "an anatomy of social and psychological survival" in post-Revolutionary Philadelphia.

Ferguson, Robert A. *Law and Letters in American Culture.* Cambridge, Mass.: Harvard University Press, 1984. Discusses Brown's works in relation to the conflict between law and literature in Brown's life and in contemporary American culture.

Fiedler, Leslie A. *Love and Death in the American Novel.* New York: Criterion Books, 1960. Discusses Brown's novels—most particularly *Edgar Huntly* —in terms of the Sentimental and Gothic traditions but not always accurate in detail; strongly colored by Fiedler's critical assumptions.

Grabo, Norman S. *The Coincidental Art of Charles Brockden Brown.* Chapel Hill: University of North Carolina Press, 1981. Analyzes the fiction in detail to argue that coincidence and doubling are central to Brown's art.

Hagenbüchle, Roland. "American Literature and the Nineteenth-Century Crisis in Epistemology: The Example of Charles Brockden Brown." *Early American Literature* 23 (1988):121–51. Reads Brown's works, and especially *Wieland,* as the first products of an epistemological crisis that was to characterize American literature throughout the nineteenth century and give it its native quality.

Hedges, William. "Charles Brockden Brown and the Culture of Contradictions." *Early American Literature* 9 (1974):107–42. Discusses Brown's novels in terms of the contradictions apparent in American culture during the 1790s.

Kimball, Arthur. *Rational Fictions: A Study of Charles Brockden Brown.* McMinnville, Ore.: Linfield Research Institute, 1968. Examines Brown's major novels in their relation to late eighteenth-century thought and recent historical events.

Lawson-Peebles, Robert. *Landscape and Written Expression in Revolutionary America: The World Turned Upside Down.* New York: Cambridge University Press, 1988. Discusses Brown's imaginative engagement with and withdrawal from the American landscape.

Lewis, R. W. B. *The American Adam: Innocence, Tragedy, and Tradition in the Nineteenth Century.* Chicago: University of Chicago Press, 1955. Discusses *Arthur Mervyn* as an initiation story that introduces the Adam figure into American literature in the person of the hero.

Patterson, Mark R. *Authority, Autonomy, and Representation in American Literature, 1776–1865.* Princeton, N.J.: Princeton University Press, 1988. Examines Brown's novels in terms of the crisis of authority that resulted from the growing democratization of American society.

Petter, Henri. *The Early American Novel.* Columbus: Ohio State University Press, 1971. Discusses Brown's books in the context of contemporary American fiction, 1775–1820.

Ringe, Donald A. *American Gothic: Imagination and Reason in Nineteenth-

Century Fiction. Lexington: University Press of Kentucky, 1982. Discusses Brown's use "of the Gothic mode as a vehicle for psychological themes."

———. "Charles Brockden Brown." In *Major Writers of Early American Literature.* Edited by Everett Emerson. Madison: University of Wisconsin Press, 1972. Discusses Brown's novels in relation to the sentimental romance, the Gothic tale, and the novel of purpose.

Samuels, Shirley. "Plague and Politics in 1793: *Arthur Mervyn.*" *Criticism* 27 (1985):225–46. Shows that in *Arthur Mervyn* the threats to society posed by "revolution, contagion, and political and sexual infidelity" are countered by the "institutions of social order," especially marriage and the family.

Slotkin, Richard. *Regeneration through Violence: The Mythology of the American Frontier, 1600–1860.* Middletown, Conn.: Wesleyan University Press, 1973. Contrasts Brown's handling of frontier materials with that of Chateaubriand to show the psychological and mythic implications of Edgar Huntly's wilderness experience.

Tompkins, Jane. *Sensational Designs: The Cultural Work of American Fiction, 1790–1860.* New York: Oxford University Press, 1985. Reads *Wieland* and *Arthur Mervyn* as commentaries on the social and political issues of the age in which they were written.

Voloshin, Beverly R. "*Edgar Huntly* and the Coherence of the Self." *Early American Literature* 23 (1988):262–80. Shows that in *Edgar Huntly* Brown both calls "into question the coherence of the external world" and undermines "the Lockean model of the linear, self-present self" as consciousness.

Wallace, James D. *Early Cooper and His Audience.* New York: Columbia University Press, 1986. Includes a chapter detailing the circumstances that prevented Brown from finding an audience for his fiction.

Ziff, Larzer. "A Reading of *Wieland.*" *PMLA* 77 (1962):51–57. Maintains that in turning away from some of the presuppositions of his age, Brown, in *Wieland,* foreshadows both "the theme and the manner" of subsequent American fiction.

Index

Characters in the novels are not included here unless referred to in discussions other than those of the specific novels in which they appear.

The Author

Born in New Orleans in 1923, Donald A. Ringe received his B.A. and M.A. from Tulane University and his Ph.D. from Harvard. He has taught at Tulane, the University of Michigan, and since 1965 the University of Kentucky, where he is professor of English. He was the College of Arts and Sciences Distinguished Professor for 1988–89. In addition to many articles and reviews that have appeared in such journals as *PMLA, American Literature, American Quarterly,* and *Nineteenth-Century Fiction,* he has published *James Fenimore Cooper* (1962; updated edition 1988), *The Pictorial Mode: Space and Time in the Art of Bryant, Irving and Cooper* (1971), and *American Gothic: Imagination and Reason in Nineteenth-Century Fiction* (1982). He serves on the editorial board for the State University of New York edition of *The Writings of James Fenimore Cooper,* for which, with his late wife, he prepared an edition of *Lionel Lincoln* (1984). He was also a member of the editorial project for the bicentennial edition of *The Novels and Related Works of Charles Brockden Brown,* for which he wrote the historical essay for *Clara Howard* and *Jane Talbot* (1986). From 1986 to 1989 he served a four-year term on the board of editors of *American Literature.*